the prevention
of juvenile delinquency

Walter C. Reckless

Simon Dinitz

THE

PREVENTION OF

JUVENILE

DELINQUENCY

an experiment

OHIO STATE UNIVERSITY PRESS
COLUMBUS   1972

Library of Congress Cataloging in Publication Data

Reckless, Walter Cade.
   The Prevention of juvenile delinquency.

   Chiefly based on a report of the Ohio State University Research
Foundation to the National Institute of Mental Health, May 31,
1970.
   1. Juvenile delinquency. I. Dinitz, Simon, joint author. II. Ohio.
State University, Columbus. Research Foundation. III. Title.
HV9069.R413   364.36   72–6750
ISBN 0–8142–0182–2

Contents

List of Tables

List of Tables : : ix

Acknowledgments

The Prevention of Juvenile Delinquency: An Experiment has been a fifteen-year odyssey involving not only the authors, their collaborators, research associates, graduate students and assistants but several cities, their educational administrators, teachers, and, not least, several thousand students. This adventure in delinquency prevention and control has had four distinct phases:

1. The "good" boy–"bad" boy phase during which we developed our theory of the self-concept as an insulator against delinquency and tested this approach in a series of longitudinal and cross-sectional studies in Columbus and Akron, Ohio and in Brooklyn, New York.

2. The development of a school-based delinquency prevention program at the sixth-grade level in selected elementary schools in Columbus.

3. The implementation of this program in all inner-

city junior high schools at the seventh-grade level using experimental, control, and comparison students.

4. The evaluation of this school-based program through an annual follow-up of all participating students and subsequent home interviews with a sample of experimental group students.

The first phase was supported continuously by the Ohio State University Office of Research and by supplemental grants from the Ohio State University Development Fund. Without these seed monies and, particularly, without the faith of the former vice-president for research, Dr. Alfred Garrett, this program would never have been implemented. We are also grateful to John Fullen, Russell Campbell, and William Heim of the Development Fund for their moral, no less than their financial, help.

Three separate research grants from the National Institute of Mental Helath supported the experimental and demonstration program and its subsequent evaluation. Without these grants, 1-R11 MH 1304 (1963–66), 5 R11 MH 02353 (1966–68) and 5 R 01 MH 14800 (1968–70), this work would certainly have been impossible to undertake and complete. We are greatly indebted to NIMH and especially to Mr. Edward Flynn for this funding.

Although the Brooklyn, New York, and Akron school systems permitted us the freedom of their classrooms and the participation of their sixth-grade students and teachers in 1959 and 1960, nearly all of our work was done in the Columbus schools. To the members of the Columbus Board of Education, the former superintendent, Dr. Harold Eibling, Mr. W. W. Miller (now retired) and Mr. L. W. Huber, assistant superintendent of instruction as well as to Mr. Herbert Williams (retired) and Miss Hortensia Dyer, we owe our deepest thanks for their cooperation.

We are grateful, too, to the principals and sixth-grade teachers in at least 44 elementary schools in Columbus for their candidate nominations and advice and counsel. It was the initiative of several of the principals that prompted us to expand the program from the four elementary schools to the seventh grade of all inner-city junior high schools. No less helpful were the personnel in the records office of the Columbus Public Schools and the officers and staff in the Juvenile Aid Bureau of the Columbus Police Department.

At the outset, the "good" boy–"bad" boy project was staffed almost exclusively by our then graduate students: Ellen Murray, Barbara Kay, Jon Simpson, Frank Scarpitti, Judson Landis, Edwin Lively, and the late Ernest Donald.

For the demonstration and later evaluation phases, we were unusually fortunate in attracting the innovative and enormously dedicated research directors of the program. Dr. Nason P. Hall was the first of our three directors (1963–66), Dr. Joseph E. Lowe, Jr. followed in 1966–68, and Craig H. Mosier II helped direct the completion of this pioneering work in 1968–70. To each of these research directors we owe a very special debt of gratitude.

The research directors were fortunate in being able to work with a group of teachers whose interest in the program, concern for their students, and personal style was truly remarkable. We can never thank them sufficiently for their willingness to work in a demonstration program that asked so much of them and gave them so relatively little in return. Teachers of the caliber of Ellsworth R. Foreman, John Hilliard,

Wayne C. Murphy, Donald L. Pierce, and Norman Landry make innovation possible and research rewarding.

Two former graduate students, Margaret Zahn and Gordon Waldo, were competent and conscientious research associates and contributed significantly to the development of our evaluation measures; other graduate students, Harry Allen, Susan Ward, Brenda Ripper, and Christine Schultz, were involved in the school and police record clearances, and Harry Allen also worked diligently on the analysis of the data.

We are grateful to three of our former project teachers, John Hillard, Wayne Murphy, and Donald Pierce, who also served as our experimental group follow-up interviewers.

Four full-time secretaries were involved in the demonstration and evaluation projects: Carma K. Hackenbracht, Judity A. Wesner, Sue J. Finley, and Patricia M. Mosure. All rate our thanks for their sincere and competent efforts. Our part-time secretaries over the years were Judy E. Gibson, Constance G. Halbe, and Jean L. Henne.

Finally, and with very special thanks, we acknowledge the contribution of Dr. W. Hugh Missildine, who was consulting psychiatrist on the project during the years 1963–66. Dr. Missildine contributed to the mental health of everyone on the project.

In addition to the large number of articles that have been published by us on our self-concept and "good" and "bad" boy studies through the years, and the two articles by Nason Hall and Gordon Waldo that are referred to in the book, the project yielded a masters thesis by Margaret Zahn and a doctoral dissertation by Gordon Waldo.

Our final report, Youth Development Project, was submitted to the National Institute of Mental Health on May 31, 1970, by the Ohio State University Research Foundation. Most of the material in this volume is taken from that final report. Another report, Youth Development Report: Curriculum, Lesson Plans and Supplementary Materials, was written by Nason Hall and the project teachers and mimeographed by the Ohio State Research Foundation in 1964. Again, some of the descriptions and discussion of the contents of our intervention program are drawn from this report.

We also gratefully acknowledge the permission of the University of Delaware to include as the Introduction an expanded and revised version of a paper presented in the series of E. E. Paul du Pont Lectures on Crime, Delinquency, and Corrections and published in *The Threat of Crime in America* in 1969.

the prevention
of juvenile delinquency

Introduction

Almost all languages in the world now include some word or phrase to designate juvenile delinquency. A few even contain a label for the middle-class delinquent, such as *blousons dores* (jackets of gold) in France, to distinguish them from those of lower class origin, the *blousons noirs* (black jackets). Israel is concerned with its *B'nei tovim* (middle-class delinquents), as well as with the more common, lower socioeconomic types of delinquents—at either level or both, a problem historically alien to Jewish life.[1] In Holland, Sweden, Italy, Poland, Russia, England and on other continents, the ever-present juvenile delinquents are referred to by various descriptive phrases, ranging from the tight-jacketed ones to hooligans and include *taipau* (Formosa), *taiyozuku* (Japan), and *tapkaroschi* (Yugoslavia).[2]

This near universality of societal concern with youthful offenders provides ample testimony that juvenile delinquency is, if not a specific concomitant, certainly an important aspect of the increasing urbanization, industrialization, modernization, and social development of nations around the world. The specific forms and types of delinquency may be as good a measure as we have of the affluence of the country. Vandalism and auto theft are particularly appropriate illustrations of this point. A recent visitor to the United States from an eastern European country was describing somewhat boastfully the enormous economic strides being made in his country. As evidence, he commented that joyriding by juveniles was the fastest growing crime and that their car theft rates might soon rival those in the United States.

\ Although juvenile delinquency is distinctly a phenomenon of modern society, history records that every age and period had its problems in controlling, socializing, and transmitting the cultural heritage to children. Mosaic law, for example, contained extreme punishments for wayward and refractory youngsters. Roman law was no less strict, endowing the family head with all manner of disciplines. Medieval usage provided for severe punishment for juvenile offenders, and the American colonial period was characterized by the specification of controls and penalties for evil children. The principal difference between these earlier periods and the present is that the youngster, except in the rarest of instances, was highly integrated into the family and the community, making the exercise of these formal sanctions largely unnecessary./

Children were employed at an early age in productive activities usually under the direct supervision and control of the family head. Responsibility and maturity came early. Marriage, family responsibilities, religious traditions, and a lack of mobility that restricted persons from birth to death to a territory having a fifty-mile radius all mitigated against delinquency. Intergenerational conflict, by no means absent, was effectively muted. The peer groups consisted of family members and neighbors; and the youth culture, subculture, and contraculture were still to be invented.

Further, there were institutional outlets and safety valves for the misfits or the deviants of those times. One could usually enlist, first under the lords or churchly patrons and, later, as nation-states emerged, in the armies and navies of nation-states. In America, until very recently, as elsewhere even now, migration provided the safety valve. The restless could roam and explore, fight and pioneer, and achieve status and renown in the process. But these institutional pathways are now largely gone. The Armed Forces are ever more demanding in their requirements, and the modern explorers are college educated and highly skilled. There is no place to run, because opportunities are tied not to geography but to education and socioeconomic status.

Urban industrial societies, by their very nature, are increasingly intolerant of deviation. Waywardness, indolence, eccentricity, and the absence of long-range goals, to say nothing of vandalism, theft, physical damage, and personal injury, are seriously disruptive and costly. As society becomes more complex, the adolescent or adult who presents problems to the system is labeled and tagged and warehoused. There is no room and little sympathy for the marginal, the disruptive, and the dependent. Although a mother may love a defective child, the family protect him, and neighbors tolerate him, the community can only put him away. This increasing intolerance of deviation accounts for the reliance upon agencies of social control to deal with any and all difficult members. Additionally, complex societies need and demand ever higher standards of competence in their members. School becomes tougher; the pressures, greater; the choice of a college, more traumatic; good grades, more imperative. For the majority who can master and exceed these demands, there is little or no problem except that of self-imposed stress. For the boy of low socioeconomic status or of lower IQ and achievement potential, the pressures and legitimate prospects may be grim as he perceives and rejects them.

CRIME AND YOUTH

The most important characteristic of the crime problem in America is the fact that crime is a youthful preoccupation.

Quite apart from the enormous amount of hidden delinquency, the number of those officially involved is staggering. Based on the estimates of a variety of sources—the *Uniform Crime Reports*, juvenile court records—a large number of adolescents aged 10 through 17 are brought to and processed by the juvenile courts annually. In 1970 the approximate figure was 1,052,000 cases (907,000 different adolescents), and these youths represented 2.8 percent of the 10 through 17 age-group in our population.[3] In addition, and based on the rule of thumb that there are four police contacts that are disposed of by the Juvenile Aid Bureaus in police departments for every case referred to court, nearly four million adolescents become known to the police each year for nontraffic offenses.

In 1970, juveniles, defined as those under 18 years

of age, constituted about 10.5 percent of all the arrests for murder and non-negligent manslaughter, 20.8 percent of the arrests for forcible rape, 33.4 percent for robbery, 50.7 percent for larceny, and 56.1 percent for auto theft.[4]

In human rather than in these percentage terms, the incredible problem of juvenile delinquency is best underscored by noting that children aged 10 and younger constituted nearly 33,000 of the arrests made for the seven major Crime Index offenses in 1970. At ages 11 and 12 about 64,000 youngsters were arrested. At ages 13 and 14, the total was 160,000. Some 113,000 adolescents aged 15 were picked up for major crimes. The single peak age was 16 in 1970; at age 16, the number of arrestees was 115,000. A sharp reduction occurred at age 17, when only 101,000 arrests were made. By age 18, the number was 89,000. It was 70,000 at age 19, 56,000 at age 20, and 49,000 at age 21.[5]

The President's Commission on Law Enforcement and Administration of Justice recently estimated that by 1975 about 25.1 percent of the boys reaching age 18 will have been arrested for a nontraffic offense, and 6.5 percent of the girls reaching age 18 will probably have experienced an arrest.

THE JUVENILE COURT CASES

❧ The million or more adolescents placed under the jurisdiction of juvenile courts in the United States are of two types. The majority consists of those whose acts would have been criminal if committed by adults. The second and smaller group, consisting of about one-fourth or less of all juvenile court cases, is composed of adolescents who have not committed any such offenses. Instead, some have violated laws such as truancy and curfew restrictions that apply specifically to children, and the rest have violated no laws at all but have been referred to the court as incorrigible, ungovernable minors in need of supervision, and as being beyond control. Surprisingly, the same outcomes, including institutionalization, sometimes occur in these latter cases as in the cases of juveniles who have engaged in serious criminal violations. This means that many youngsters are drawn into the correctional system who should be dealt with in a health and welfare rather than a criminal context. One reasonable way of solving this problem and eliminating the stigma customarily conferred on juvenile violators would be to limit the jurisdiction of the court to adolescents who have broken laws applicable to persons at all ages. All other youngsters could then be referred to other more appropriate public and private agencies, particularly mental health clinics and outpatient facilities./If this were done, over half the girls presently referred to the court would no longer be subject to its jurisdiction. Similarly, one fifth of the boys would also be treated elsewhere.

The Scandinavian countries have led the way in handling delinquent adolescents under 14 years of age in a welfare context.\In the recent Supreme Court decision *In re Gault*, which is a landmark signaling a change in direction, the Court held that, in addition to the rights of due process to be accorded juveniles, the court cannot impose any supervision or sanctions upon a child unless he has been found guilty of the offense charged. By extension and implication then, unless a petition or affidavit alleging delinquency is filed, the case should be handled by a noncourt agency. So-called unofficial cases will have no place in court./

SOCIAL CHANGE AND DELINQUENCY

It is one thing to describe the near universality of juvenile delinquency in industrial and even in developing societies and to explore its various attributes including court processing but is quite another to explain the etiology of juvenile involvement in crime. Various interpretations are usually offered ranging from those that focus on moral decay to those on the other end of the continuum that emphasize biological, psychological, and psychiatric problems as the basis for maladaptive conduct. There is, of course, no specific explanation, in the usual sense of that word, for delinquency. Instead, \it is necessary to view delinquency, and more broadly, various other forms of deviancy, as inherently a part of our social system. To prevent and control the problem, substantial alterations in the social structure would be required—changes few of us would be willing to accept. Delinquency, along with other social pathologies, is the stiff price exacted for the modern, affluent, twentieth-century life style.

This twentieth-century life style is a product of a series of silent revolutions. These revolutions have transformed the very fabric of human existence, challenged historic moral and ethical values, induced the creation of new philosophies such as pragmatism and existentialism, and more profoundly affected the history and destiny of man than all of the violent revolutions ever recorded.[6]

Without belaboring the issue, these silent revolutions include principally the industrial, the technological, and the scientific, which have altered man's conception of the universe, of truth, of work, and of himself. They have been coupled with the mobility revolutions—both vertical and horizontal—that changed our conceptions of place and space and broke down the traditional social control imposed by family, neighborhood, and generation. The urbanization revolution in turn led to a further breakdown in the social control mechanisms so effective in the small society. Finally, together, these revolutions resulted in rising expectations, via the mass media, to the life style of persons in the most affluent of societies. Never again will people who have been so exposed settle for less. Evidence for this is found not only in the slums of America but in the most remote outposts of mankind.

The net effect of these dramatic changes or silent revolutions has been to create a condition of cultural lag in our institutions and of social disorganization in many segments of our society. The old order is dead or dying. The new one is yet to emerge. It is not by any means unfair to assert that, for a very large sector of the American people, the traditional institutional arrangements simply do not operate effectively. Age and sex roles no longer mean much. Intergenerational conflict has never been greater. Adolescence and aging are stages in the life cycle that are, by definition and expectation, traumatic. The cohesive nuclear family is becoming an oddity. Many of its functions have passed to other agencies. The educational system is excellent for those prepared to learn and grow within it. Its inadequacies and failures, for those who are not, are well documented in official reports and studies: in the dropouts, the truants, the functional illiterates, and in the self-defined failures annually produced. The religious system, once extremely effective in providing meaning and direction, has been weakened almost beyond recognition as the central focus of social control. Without the continual reinforcement of these sanctioning agencies, "norm erosion" is leaving all too many adolescents without either strong internal or external controls to guide them.

If the solution to a problem, as computer experts tell us, is asking an answerable question, then the prevention and control of delinquency depends equally on sorting out the various elements and focusing on the significant issues. These variables, alluded to at many previous points, include the family, the community, and the value structure./

THE FAMILY AND DELINQUENCY

The family, in one or another form, is a universal social institution. In every culture and in every time period, the family has developed a format consonant with and supportive of other institutions. Various typologies have described this adaptation of the family to the changing world. On one continuum the modern family has moved from an institutional to a companionship model; on another, the trustee, domestic, and atomistic stages have succeeded one another. Those with prophetic vision contend that a new, more relevant model is emerging because of the sexual revolution occasioned by medical and scientific advance. This model envisions a two-stage family: first, marriage based on idealized notions and second, after divorce, remarriage based on mature considerations of the realities and difficulties of partnership, procreation, socialization, and all the rest.

Whatever the fate of this vision and of similar trend deductions, the modern family is substantially different from its predecessors. Many of its functions—education, recreation, even to an extent socialization of the young—have been transferred to other agencies. With the passing of the family as an economic unit, patterns of familism, patriarchalism, and other elements necessary for running the family as an efficient unit are no longer meaningful. Few structures have replaced these losses, and this is the reason for the general breakdown in family functioning.

This breakdown or disorganization is reflected in a wide variety of ways. First, the divorce rate in the United States has climbed precipitously since the turn of the century. In 1900 there were about 8 divorces for every 100 marriages annually. The percentage at present is about 25. This means that at least 400,000 marriages are terminated each year by divorce and 100,-000 by desertion and other forms of separation. Fully half of these divorces occur in the first half-dozen years of marriage. Since 97 percent of those divorced remarry, the disillusionment is not with marriage as such but with the specific partner. Again, wholly as an aside, a divorced woman has a greater probability of remarrying than does a single woman of marrying for the first time. With the decline in family size, and the general exercise of willful control over births, only two-fifths of the marriages that fail involve children—the one bright element in an otherwise dismal picture.

These trends have prompted many sociologists of the family to describe modern marriage as a type of successive or serial monogamy. Families may often consist of three sets of children—his, hers, and theirs. The prevalence of this pattern becomes very apparent when one tries to do longitudinal follow-up studies of school children over a five-year period or longer. The name changes are remarkably frequent. The serial monogamy type of family is becoming a new version of the old extended family.

As far as delinquency is involved, the evidence is convincing that family dissolution and, perhaps even more important, family breakdown and pathology are significantly related to juvenile delinquency, particularly at the lower-class level.[7] The consistent and impressive results of the Gluecks and of other researchers are beyond refutation. It is possible to predict the future delinquent involvement of lower-class boys in the first grade with some accuracy using only those variables that concern the cohesiveness of the family and the quality of parent-child relationships. In a very recent study, Craig and Glick of the New York City Youth Board present 10 years of information on a cohort of 301 boys entering the first grade. Of the 301, about 53 percent were rated as behavior problems at some time during elementary school by their teachers. Of the total, 257 were nondelinquent, whereas 44 became delinquent. Almost 80 percent of the delinquents and just 27.3 percent of the nondelinquents were rated as troublesome by the end of the third grade. Using the Glueck family predictive factors (supervision by mother, discipline by mother, and cohesiveness of family) as an adjunct to the teacher classification, the authors contend they could have predicted the case outcome of 92 percent of the later delinquents.[8]

A number of other evidences of the relationship of

family dissolution and pathology to delinquency might be cited. One in particular deserves serious thought. In recent studies, the so-called multiproblem families in our communities numbering somewhere between 7 and 10 percent of our city populations account for more than half of the juvenile court cases. Such families are often served by a dozen different agencies, most with indifferent effect. This hard-core pathological family challenges much of our traditional thinking and nearly all of our present practices of delivering services to persons and families in need.

The high rates of family dissolution, maladjustment, and pathology adversely affect the socialization of the young and create a cadre of adolescents who are freed of external restraint and, often, of internal control as well. Any experienced correctional administrator can attest to the changing composition of the delinquent and criminal population. Even allowing for the changes in institutional populations, attributable to the more frequent use of probation and other treatment methods, the present breed of youthful and adult inmates is increasingly beyond rehabilitation. Correctional people speak of this new breed as lacking in feeling, devoid of shame, anxiety-free, impulse-ridden, and all the rest of the attributes associated with sociopathy.[9] One plausible explanation offered for the greater frequency of these *dyysocial* and antisocial persons is inadequate socialization in the family. The unreached and unreachable ones have never established patterns of identification with anyone, making it incredibly difficult for them to feel and experience and relate except on the most primitive level. Depending on the number and specificity of the criteria, about a fourth of adult male prisoners might be classified as sociopaths.

THE EMERGENCE OF THE FEMALE-BASED HOUSEHOLD

Quite aside from the demonstrably serious consequences for normal personality development inherent in family dissolution and pathology, a new style of family organization is emerging that, less visibly but nonetheless clearly, is influencing adolescent socialization. This new pattern has been called the female-based household. The female-based household cuts across class lines, although the reasons for its existence at the different class levels vary. In the upper and upper-middle strata, the stature of the male derives not from his familial role adequacy but from his instrumental economic activities. The father is absent from the home for perfectly legitimate occupational reasons —but he is absent nevertheless. Even his leisure has become instrumental; social and recreational activity must be justified in occupational terms. Somehow it is less than manly to be concerned about home, family, and children. This pattern of family organization is rapidly filtering down to the general middle-class population with the result that family decision-making has become a female prerogative. Because of increasing education and employment in professional and white collar occupations, the pressures toward the institutionalization of the female-based household will surely grow. Part of the acknowledged increase in middle-class delinquency—vandalism, drug offenses, gambling violations and sexual offenses—has been attributed to this unique family format that has emerged.

In middle-class life even when the father is absent, or to all intents and purposes a nonparticipant in family life, at least there is a male present who plays the conventional roles. No such redeeming feature exists in many lower-class families. The one-parent family is frequently the rule with the woman, her female relatives or female neighbors playing all of the relevant family roles. Children may not know their fathers at all or may simply view the father role as a useless appendage in the family. Male life is lived on the street corner, in the bar, and among other males. A minor contributor, or none at all, the once powerful patriarchal figure is now a most unimportant person. Psychologists, educationalists, and sociologists have focused their attention on the developmental problems, learning impediments, the lack of stimulation, and other consequences of this style of family life.

Criminologists have been very concerned with the lack of a male-role model in the female-based household and its relationship to the compulsive-masculinity syndrome that is best illustrated by the adolescent gang. In fact, Bloch and Niederhoffer suggest that adolescent insecurity is the key variable in the explanation of the gang phenomenon in the urban setting. From the early research of Thrasher to the more recent work of Yablonsky, Short and Strodtbeck, Cohen, and others, the gang is depicted as offering a behavior-role-model system that is appealing to the adolescent male.[10]

The compulsive-masculinity theme, as an outgrowth of the female-based household, can be exemplified in several major themes in American life—the preoccupation with and emphasis on speed, force, and violence as major cultural motifs. The mass media have done a great deal to idealize these values. Still, it is impossible to idealize that which is not consonant with and reflective of genuine values. From the Hell's Angels, whose masculinity is tied to their dress, motorcycles, and chains, to the youngest tattooed truant on the street corner, masculinity and physical aggressiveness are tied together. The "all masculine" male takes his pleasures where and when he can. He is so much a male as to be almost a caricature of the type.

Despite this masculinity crisis that has been identified as etiologic in the formation of juvenile gangs and as a general cultural motif, it is necessary to recognize that the majority of youngsters—even those from female-dominated households—find adequate and lawful alternative solutions for their masculine identity difficulties. It is the lower-class boy who is most profoundly affected.

LOWER-CLASS FOCAL CONCERNS

There are certain universals in being lower class the world over. In addition to grinding poverty, despair, high mortality rates, poor health, hopelessness, inadequate housing, large families, underemployment and unemployment, the absence of occupational skills, and insufficient education, lower-class life tends also to feature certain values. These value or focal concerns are generated in everyday life as the poor and uneducated confront the realities of their existence.[11] Lower-class values, so dramatically depicted by Oscar Lewis, tend to reinforce the compulsive-masculinity emphasis and are themselves an important element in generating delinquent behavior by lower-class teenage boys. In the Caribbean area, for example, the ethos described by the term *machismo* (masculinity) is a central focus of concern to many men. It is perhaps the dominant concern of males at the lowest socioeconomic level. For this reason, a considerably greater proportion of Latin

American criminals than United States offenders have been involved in violent crimes: shooting, knifing, beating, and other forms of mayhem. In the United States a subculture of violence, male and lower class, has been identified by Wolfgang and by others.[12] The pattern of violence—intra-race and intra-sex—is most evident on weekends and is often triggered by casual and meaningless insults and quarrels that might go unanswered entirely, except for the United States version of *machismo*, called "being chicken" or cowardly.

Walter Miller has sounded the lower-class focal concern theme about as well as anyone. Says he:

> There is a substantial segment of present-day American society whose way of life, values and characteristic patterns of behavior are the product of a distinctive cultural system that may be termed "lower class." Evidence indicates that this cultural system is becoming increasingly distinctive, and that the size of the group that shares this tradition is increasing. The lower-class way of life, in common with that of all distinctive cultural groups, is characterized by a set of focal concerns —areas or issues that command widespread and persistent attention and a high degree of emotional involvement.[13]

The lower-class focal concerns according to Miller are trouble, toughness, smartness, excitement, fate, and autonomy. Concern over trouble is a dominant preoccupation in lower-class life. Getting into or staying out of trouble represent major issues for all categories of lower-class persons; young and old, male and female. The everyday language of lower-class boys contains an inordinate number of references to this concept. Under these circumstances, although trouble (usually with the law, teachers, principals, landlords, merchants, bosses, coworkers, and family members) may not be desired, it is certainly not unexpected.

Toughness is a second focal concern. The concept emphasizes physical prowess (not toughness and discipline of mind that are middle-class virtues), fearlessness, hardness, unemotionality, and maleness. Miller invokes a psychoanalytic explanation for the pervasiveness of this concern, but whatever its origin, a few minutes in a lower-class junior high school is sufficient to convince even the most skeptical of us that toughness is an esteemed social value for the lower-class.

Smartness, as emphasized in lower-class culture, involves the ability to con others and be immune to being conned by others. Although manipulation is not restricted to lower-class life, it is not highly valued at the middle-class level where work is extolled and is thought superior to manipulation. In addition, excitement and thrill-seeking are classic values of lower-class life. This search for novelty is evident in the widespread gambling behavior characteristic of all ages and both sexes, but to a lesser degree for females. Numbers, policy, lottery, dice, cards, and so forth are commonplace modes of taking a risk. Speed, as in drag racing on or off the track, is highly valued. Motorcycle races and activities and demolition derbies are two very interesting variations on this theme. The excitement compulsion extends to risking police detection in criminal offenses, fist fighting, running away from home and "bumming it," and to many other activities. Excitement is counterbalanced by periods of inactivity and dullness. "Hanging around" connotes the opposite of excitement. This inaction was classically phrased in a recent book as follows: "Where are you going?" "Nowhere." "What are you doing?" "Nothing."

Another important focal concern, fate, refers to the belief that hidden forces dominate and determine future events and that the person himself can do little to alter the course of events. This preoccupation is seen especially in the gambling ethos. Picking a right or lucky number is a major activity. To a greater or lesser degree, powerlessness is nearly always translated into a chance or luck ideology. The nearly universal lower-class preoccupation with jinxes and luck merely attests to the realistic assessment of life chances by the disenfranchised everywhere.

The last of the major lower-class focal concerns identified by Miller is autonomy. The concept of autonomy is found in much of the present writing about lower-class life and its deviancy-generating potential. Sometimes referred to as external restraint, the proposition is that persons at the lower reaches of the stratification system perceive themselves as, and in fact are, pushed around by others in the system with greater power. Authority is rarely seen as legitimate and is imposed from the outside. Freedom of movement and choice are perceived as severely restricted. In lower-class terminology, "Everyone is on my back." Hence the great ideological goal is to free oneself from these restraints and to be able to act independently in vital matters. As Lipset and others have suggested, the quest for independence and adulthood, so well expressed by the Negro in his warning to the police, "Don't call me 'boy'," has its origin in the authoritarianism of lower-class life. The often heavy-handed treatment accorded lower-class youngsters at home is often the start of lifelong disenchantment with every form of authority, however legitimate.

Given these values, the emergence of the delinquent

subculture as a life style in slum neighborhoods is a logical outcome. The delinquent subculture and life style provide the male adolescent with a means of expressing his maleness, of risk taking, of contesting with authority, and of creating social groups in which he can exercise autonomy. Although there are other patterns and life styles in slum areas that deflect many youngsters from criminal involvement, such as evangelistic religious sects, ethnic enclaves, character-building groups, and even strong cohesive families, the delinquency subculture is pervasively attractive to many slum boys.

To the extent that the lower-class boy feels inadequate to compete effectively in a middle-class oriented society, featuring an emphasis on education, propriety, orderliness, long-range goals, deferred gratification, and planning, his low self esteem will translate into inadequate performance and delinquent behavior.[14]

AVAILABLE OPPORTUNITY

/ Cloward and Ohlin following the Cohen and Miller tradition seek to explain delinquency in the lower classes and the existence of pressures that tend to create delinquency subcultures in terms of (1) the limited opportunity to find legitimate means to goals, and (2) the availability of illegitimate means within modern urban life.[15] The first part, limited access to legitimate means, is a take-over of Merton's revision of Durkheim's initial formulation. The second part of the theory, that is, the availability of illegitimate means to ends, argues for the reliance on criminal patterns as alternatives when legitimate avenues to success goals are closed.

Cloward and Ohlin contend that the lower-class urban youths experience great disparity between the aspirations that are culturally generated in adolescents and the chances of achieving these goals. It is the disparity between the two that generates deviant behavior—between the culturally induced aspirations and the available legitimate means for fulfilling these aspirations. In their own words, Cloward and Ohlin maintain that "the disparity between what lower-class youth are led to want and what is actually available to them is the source of a major problem of adjustment. . . . Faced with limitations on legitimate avenues of access to (conventional) goals, and unable to revise their aspirations downward, they experience intense frustrations; the exploration of nonconformist alternatives may be the result."[16]

The problems of adjustment and frustration of lower-class youth, resulting from disparity of aspirations and their chances of fulfillment, are also referred to as "position discontent." Cloward and Ohlin feel that it is very important to recognize that many lower-class youths develop this position discontent without being oriented toward the success goals of the middle class. They can experience position discontent even in terms of lower-class success goals.

In the United States with its vertical-mobility ethic, hard-core, multi-problem lower-class people are likely to experience futility in their attempts to find ways and means to success. The majority can find no legitimate way out of poverty. This view of delinquent behavior as the result of the disparity between aspirations and chances of fulfillment is a more structurally oriented thesis than is inadequate socialization or conformity to lower-class values (Miller). The frustration, disparity, position-discontent hypothesis describes delinquency as the result of pressure toward deviance. Delinquent subcultures, especially the criminal and conflict-oriented subcultures, provide illegal paths to success goals; these paths constitute a mode of adjustment or solution to the frustration dilemma or position discontent. The retreatist subculture represents an escape from competition in a world where success is unattainable.

Cloward and Ohlin recognize furthermore that there are both collective and solitary solutions to the problem of blockage or limited access to legitimate goals. If individuals attribute their failure to the social structure, to the lack of opportunities, then they are likely to seek or develop a collective solution such as a delinquent subculture. If failure is perceived as a personal failure, then individuals are likely to develop solitary solutions. In the extreme case, the attempt to cope with personal failure can result in mental illness.

The Cloward-Ohlin theory attempts to fuse together four interrelated components: (1) two differential opportunity systems (legal and illegal) in American urban society; (2) blocked aspirations (culturally induced) within the available legitimate means to ends (the legitimate structure) that lead to "position discontent"; (3) the generation of a delinquency subculture as a collective solution by lower-class youth for overcoming blocked aspirations; and (4) the withdrawal of legitimacy from the conventional and the attribution of legitimacy to illegal means to achieve socially acceptable goals.

A NEW FOCUS

Despite the elegance of these and related structural and, particularly, subcultural themes now dominating the criminological literature, this approach has failed singularly to account for the obvious fact that most adolescents, even in the highest delinquency areas, manage to avoid any involvement with the juvenile justice system. Thus, it is no longer sufficient or sensible for criminologists to call attention only to the adverse impact of disorganized and disadvantaged neighborhoods, family tensions and inadequacies, peer pressures to deviate, street corner societies, and the structural impediments to the achievement of socially desirable goals. Who responds to patterns of deviance and delinquency? Who resists and adopts non-deviant coping mechanisms?

In a fluid world, the sociological core of criminologists must search for self factors that have a containing potential or a potential to steer the person away from risks and deviance. For example, a good self-concept certainly has the power of appropriate self-direction, steering the individual away from bad associates, cheating, misappropriation of other persons' money, drug abuse, overuse of alcohol, and other violations of moral and legal norms. Likewise, good role models that have been internalized also have the capacity to direct the person toward acceptable activities.

The emphasis upon implanting and reinforcing factors of internal containment appears to be the best rationale for effective child rearing, education, and delinquency prevention. In fact, it was this containment emphasis in the study of delinquent behavior that led the authors to develop the project described in this volume which is a delinquency prevention program in the inner city focusing upon boys at the beginning of adolescence. Not only was it felt that there should be an experimental test of appropriate preventive programs but it was felt also that such a preventive effort should focus upon the buildup of inner strengths in preadolescent boys of the slums who are also showing signs of gravitating toward delinquency. This is what the present volume is all about.

1. Shlomo Shoham and M. Hovav, "B'nei Tovim—Middle and Upper Class Delinquency in Israel," *Sociology and Social Research* 48 (July 1964) :4.

2. William C. Kvaraceus, "Juvenile Delinquency: A Problem for the Modern World," *Federal Probation* 28 (September 1964): 12–18.

3. *Juvenile Court Statistics, 1970* (Washington, D.C.: U.S. Department of Health, Education, and Welfare, January 7, 1972), p. 2.

4. *Uniform Crime Reports, 1970* (Washington, D.C.: U.S. Department of Justice, August 31, 1971), table 29, p. 128.

5. Ibid., table 28, pp. 126–27.

6. Russell R. Dynes et al., *Social Problems: Dissensus and Deviation in an Industrial Society* (New York: Oxford University Press, 1964), pp. 18–45.

7. For an excellent review of the research on this subject, see Hyman Rodman and Paul Grams, "Juvenile Delinquency and the Family: A Review and Discussion" in *Juvenile Delinquency, and Youth Crime*, Task Force on Juvenile Delinquency, The President's Commission on Law Enforcement and Administration of Justice, 1967, Appendix L, pp. 188–222.

8. Maude M. Craig and Selma Glick, "School Behavior Related to Later Delinquency and Non-Delinquency" *Criminologica* 5 (February 1968) :17–27.

9. Robert D. Hare, *Psychopathy: Theory and Research* (New York: Wiley, 1970).

10. Walter C. Reckless, *The Crime Problem*, 4th edition (New York: Appleton-Century-Crofts, 1967), chapter 19.

11. Walter P. Miller, "Lower Class Culture as a Generating Milieu of Gang Delinquency," *Journal of Social Issues* 14 (1958): 5–19.

12. Marvin E. Wolfgang and Franco Ferracuti, *The Subculture of Violence* (London: Tavistock, 1967) ; Marvin E. Wolfgang, *Patterns in Criminal Homicide* (Philadelphia; University of Pennsylvania Press, 1958).

13. Miller, "Lower Class Culture," p. 7.

14. Albert K. Cohen, *Delinquent Boys: The Culture of The Gang* (New York: Free Press, 1955).

15. Richard A. Cloward and Lloyd E. Ohlin, *Delinquency and Opportunity: A Theory of Delinquent Groups* (New York: Free Press, 1960).

16. Ibid., p. 86.

CHAPTER ONE

An Overview of
Juvenile Delinquency

Only in the last one hundred and fifty years has modern society developed a special concern for the juvenile offender. Throughout history, he was treated as a common criminal when his violational behavior was serious enough to warrant action. History does not record the number of young people under 14 or 16 years of age who were burned at the stake, hung from the scaffold, or lashed with a whip in public. There is no evidence of the prevalence of young male offenders (they would now be considered juvenile delinquents) who were transported in the eighteenth and nineteenth centuries to far-off places under the so-called system of transportation, which had been substituted for hanging. Likewise, no specific indications are given in regard to the relative number of young as compared with mature male offenders who were chained on the galley ships of the Roman Empire.

/ It is clear that three major trends developed in the nineteenth and twentieth centuries that had great bearing on the handling of juvenile offenders and on the increasing involvement of young people in deviant behavior. The first trend resulted from a movement to separate the handling of the juvenile from the handling of the adult offender. The second trend represented a growing extension of the period between adolescence and adulthood, which eventually resulted in the breakdown of an unambiguous role structure for youth. The third trend developed in the wake of increased mobility and fluidity of the population in modern countries, causing considerable alienation of youths as well as adults from their original social bases.\

THE MOVEMENT TOWARD SEPARATE HANDLING

\In regard to the first trend, there were two or three early attempts in Europe to establish and operate specially organized institutions for delinquent boys. With the advent of the nineteenth century, the movement toward handling delinquents separate from adults began to take hold, not only in the United States but also in Europe.\The initial efforts to separate the two focused on the building of so-called reform schools for delinquent youths. The state of New York established a separate institution for committed young male offenders in the 1820s.\Other states in the United States soon followed suit. For example, Ohio founded its separate reform school for delinquent boys in 1856, patterned after an institution that had been operating a few years earlier in France.

Through the intercession of a Boston shoemaker, John Augustus, judicial clemency was extended by the court in Boston to young offenders and to alcoholics, beginning in 1841. John Augustus, a public spirited, if somewhat impecunious citizen, voluntarily embarked on a career of bailing out youths, prostitutes, and drunks from the Boston Municipal Court. He thus became the court's unofficial probation officer. After carefully selecting his candidates, he bailed them out, made them pledge their good conduct, and often provided them with lodging. He proselytized employers for jobs and physicians for medical care for his "probationers." After his death, the Massachusetts legislature authorized a state visiting agency for the placement of juveniles on probation. This allowed the courts to withhold commitment to an institution and to permit supervision of the offender by an interested citizen, family, or agency known to the court. Thus, the idea of probation as a substitute for commitment began. Shortly after the Civil War, probation laws began to be passed in the various states legalizing the use of suspended sentences (probation).

Somewhat later, about 1880, a movement developed to separate juveniles from adults in jails, founded on the theory as well as the fact that young offenders were often contaminated and exploited (sexually) by being placed in the same cells with adult offenders. This movement eventually led to the establishment of special detention homes in the large urban counties for juvenile delinquents awaiting trial.

The final development in separate handling came with the movement that established separate court procedure for juvenile delinquents and, in large cities, separate juvenile courts. The state of Illinois led the field in this endeavor with the passage of a law in 1899 prescribing a different procedure for processing juvenile cases and also establishing the first juvenile court in the United States, located in Cook County (Chicago). Actually, the trend toward separate handling reflected the growing concern of an enlightened public about the deleterious effects of the mixture of juvenile and adults at the police, detention, court, and institutional levels. In the last generation, the movement toward special treatment reached the police departments of the large cities, which established juvenile bureaus to process juvenile cases separately from adult arrestees.

EXTENDED ADOLESCENCE

The second major trend followed as a sort of aftermath to the Industrial Revolution. The preindustrialized period of European and American history found the 14-year-old boy being placed as an apprentice, to learn a trade and to become a journeyman artisan at 18 years of age. He was encouraged to marry early— a girl was frequently married off by her father at 14 years of age. In other words, the role structure of preindustrialized modern society made provisions for the youth to mature early and to assume economic, social, religious, marital, and parental responsibilities.

/ With the passage of time following the Industrial Revolution, fewer boys went through the apprenticeship system, and fewer girls were married at 14. And more and more, youth found difficulty in finding rewarding employment. Assisting the delay in social maturation, compulsory school attendance laws were passed in the United States, at first compelling attendance until 14 years of age and later until 16 years of age. With the advancement in compulsory school attendance laws, more and more youths continued in high school until 18 years of age; and more and more youths in the United States went on to college for still another 4 years. One might say that the "growing-up" period in American life was definitely extended several years beyond what it had been in Benjamin Franklin's day/

LACK OF ROLE STRUCTURE AND DELAYED MATURATION

It appears that the social system in the United States today delays the maturation process and that American society has really lost its role structure for youth. There is nothing for them to do. The labor unions will not have them. Industry does not want them. The marriage laws, except in special instances, prevent them from marrying under 18 or 21 years of age (although they are permitted to get a driver's license at 16 or 18). In most cities and states they are not legally permitted to buy or to consume intoxicating beverages. Along with this trend toward delayed social maturation, most states have extended the age limit of their juvenile court laws to 18 years of age. One or two still retain 16 as the limit, and one state has a special provision for handling youths up to 21 years of age.

MOBILITY, FLUIDITY, AND ALIENATION

/In addition to lack of a role structure in which youth under 18 can mature and in addition to the consequent delay in maturation, American society has been affected by all the undermining consequences of the great mobility of its population and the exaggerated fluidity of life, including the enormous spread of new patterns of behavior through the mass media, especially television.\The breakdown of the local neighborhood life and the dwindling effective control of the family over its young members have been both the cause and effect of this mobility and fluidity. Furthermore, a trend toward alienation (detachment) of young people (as well as adults) from families, schools, organizations, and religion also has come about, consequent for the most part to increasing urbanization and technology.

EXPERIMENTATION AND REVOLT AS PATHWAYS

/ Certainly, the present situation is ripe for all kinds of experimentation in behavior by young people: sex, drugs, vandalism, theft, burglary, auto theft, and so forth. The American scene, especially in urban areas is ripe also for revolt of young people against lingering controls of the so-called establishment. Hence, the breakdown in the role structure for young people (nothing for them to do to help them grow up) plus the alienating effects of increased mobility and fluidity represent the major pathways into delinquency and crime in the United States today./

THE POTENTIAL OF SEPARATE HANDLING

Can this concern for separate handling of the juvenile offender—separate from the adult offender at police, court, and institutional levels—provide adequate methods for dealing with youthful offenders today and for guiding them back to a more conforming course of life and behavior? The answer is yes, if our society can develop the effective police work with juveniles under 18 years of age, effective juvenile courts (including probation service), and effective retraining and preparation for adult life at the institutions for committed juvenile delinquents. The answer is also yes, if a large segment of the American public is at the same time able to overcome its labeling and stigmatizing of juvenile offenders.

The main potential of separate handling of the juvenile offender who comes to the attention of the police, the court, and the institution is in providing him with an opportunity to assume acceptable behavior patterns to avoid future involvement in delinquency. Separate handling is nowhere near as certain a cure for delinquency as is most of medical treatment for disease. But it is certainly an opportunity for the young person to develop internal controls and to settle down.

THE TASK OF PREVENTION

On the other hand, prevention of juvenile delinquency in modern America must be geared to overcoming the lack of a meaningful role structure for young people as well as overcoming the trend toward alienation and revolt. The creation of a more meaningful role structure will have to evolve from appropriate changes in the social system. Supplementary to the evolution of a better role structure for youth is the need for young persons themselves to develop inner controls that are capable of steering them away from pitfalls. The internalization of inner controls is something that psychiatrists, psychologists, social workers, teachers, and ministers are trying to facilitate in pre-adolescent and early adolescent youths. Such an effort is truly preventive of delinquent and deviant behavior, especially in a fluid world of alienated individuals. The present project is concerned with the possible internalization of feasible role models as an ingredient of self-control.

CHAPTER TWO

Basic Dimensions of Juvenile Delinquency

In order to understand the point at which delinquency prevention programs have been attempted in the United States as well as to assess their preventive potential, it is important to set forth the basic dimensions of the juvenile delinquency problem.

SOCIAL AND LEGAL DEFINITIONS

First of all, juvenile delinquency is a socially and a legally defined behavior problem. As behavior, delinquency falls in the area of deviancy—behavior that is contrary to the prevailing social norms and that arouses public as well as individual concern. Supporting the deviancy aspect of delinquency is the legal aspect—the definitions of delinquent behavior and the definitions of the age limits of a juvenile delinquent.

In regard to the latter, the special laws in most states of the United States define juvenile delinquency as a violation of any section of the criminal code by a young

person under 18 years of age plus certain violations
that do not apply to adults, such as running away from
home, truancy from school, incorrigibility, and so
forth/One or two states still keep the upper age limit
at 16 years of age, where it was originally set in 1899
by the first juvenile court law in the state of Illinois.
The lower age limit of juvenile delinquency has never
been set by law but has been taken over from the English common law, which held that no child under 7
years of age could be held legally responsible.

AGE AND SEX DISTRIBUTION

Actually, very few children under 12 years of age
are reported to the police or referred to the juvenile
courts or to the courts holding juvenile sessions. Evi-
dently, preadolescent children do not manifest very
much violational behavior, or the victims and observers
of their behavior do not report it to official sources. Beginning with 12 years of age, the age curve of delinquency begins to rise precipitously, reaching its peak
at 16 or 17 years of age. During adolescence, the child
in America is participating more outside the home and
is being influenced more and more by companions, prevailing patterns of youthful behavior, and community
conditions.

Of the total number of arrests in 1970, as reported
by 5,270 police agencies serving about three-quarters
of the population in the United States, 9.2 percent were
under 15 years of age and 25.3 were under 18 years of
age.[1] In proportion to adult arrests (18 years and
over), the largest number of juvenile arrests, as
booked by the police, were for the offenses of burglary,

larceny, arson, vandalism, curfew violations, and running away from home and school.

In 4,222 police agencies, covering about two-thirds of the population of the United States, 1,182,666 males and 321,736 females under 18 years of age were arrested in 1970, making a ratio of less than 4 to 1.[2] The 1969 statistics from 491 juvenile courts in the country reported a boy-girl ratio of 3 to 1 for the year.[3] As of June 30, 1970,[4] the ratio of boys to girls was approximately the same for the youths who had been committed to public institutions for delinquents. One should note that the ratio of girls to boys at the police, court, and institutional levels is several times higher than similar ratios for adult offenders. The adult male to female ratio is approximately 8 to 1 for all offenses, and for the major theft offenses 20 to 1 or even 30 to 1. As for incarceration, the male to female ratio is even higher. In Ohio, for example, of the 9,200 inmates in all prisons in early 1972, only 260 were women. Similarly, while jails and workhouses are desperately overcrowded, the female counterparts or units are virtually empty by comparison. The county workhouse for females in Franklin County (Columbus) is filled to approximately one-third capacity.

The adolescent girl proportionately enters the delinquency arena much more than the adult woman enters the criminal arena, reflecting, among other things, public concern about girls and the fear that waywardness will lead to pregnancy and venereal disease. This protectiveness continues despite the changes in sexual standards and the greater freedom now accorded young persons, including girls. If the United States had the same public attitude and the same juvenile justice system as Switzerland, for example, the wayward girl would not be handled by the police, the juvenile courts, or public institutions, but would be left alone by the official agencies. Then her ratio to male juvenile offenders would drop considerably; and instead of being 4 to 1 or 3 to 1, the ratio might even become 15 to 1, thus approximating the adult ratio.

REPORTING AND REFERRAL

There are very few crimes or delinquencies that are seen ("on view") by patrolmen; and hence, there are very few instances of delinquent behavior that are acted upon as they take place. Once in a while, foot patrolmen or squad-car patrolmen might happen upon a violation as it is taking place. Delinquent behavior, then, as in the case of criminal behavior, is principally reported by victims. Sometimes, it is reported by observers or bystanders, but not often. Consequently, delinquency is a function of the complaining process— the willingness of the victim or observer to call the police (or, sometimes, to notify the juvenile court directly).

After the complaint comes to the attention of the police, an investigation is made. This is followed by a decision on the part of the investigating officers to hold or to not hold the delinquent for the juvenile court. If the youth is not held, he is often warned, and his parents are warned by the police about the consequences of future involvement.

COURT ACTION

If and when an adolescent is held for the juvenile court, he may be allowed to go home and await further processing or he may be placed in a detention facility for delinquents. The juvenile courts in the large cities usually have an intake procedure that screens the cases. If the intake officer of the court feels that the youth can be allowed to go home without further processing, this finishes the procedure. But if the intake worker feels that the case should come before the judge or his referee, then an affadavit must be filed (by the police or any other complainant). The child and his parents are notified of what to expect in the court procedure and are told that they have a right to be represented in the proceeding by counsel (*in re* of the Gault decision).

The cases that are held for a court hearing may be placed on probation to the court or may be committed to a state or private institution. Only seldom are the cases that are held for a hearing discharged without some action or without being found "not guilty." One must realize that the overwhelming majority of counties in the United States merely have a special hearing in regular courts for juvenile cases—perhaps on Fridays or some other designated time. They do not have intake screening by an intake officer, and they do not have referees acting as judges. Nevertheless, the court procedure represents a hearing, in which the complainant can be present or the affadavit is read out in court. The child and his parents may have the opportunity to give some particulars of rebuttal. Both in regular courts and in the specially organized juvenile courts, there are few instances in which the child is actually represented by counsel.

UNREPORTED DELINQUENCY

There is no question that the largest volume of delinquency does not come to the attention of the police or the courts, for reasons noted above. Victims or observers seldom complain, and because much of it is hidden from view, the police rarely see it actually taking place. Sociologists have tried to obtain some gauge of unreported and unacted-upon delinquency from sample studies of so-called self-reporting.[5] The indications are that the amount of involvement is considerable for youths who do not come to the attention of the police and the courts as well as for those who do—somewhat more for the latter than the former.

One of the most recent studies of self-reported delinquent behavior revealed that most of the "high violators" in the sample of seventh- , eighth- , and ninth-grade boys in a large city in New York state, did not appear in the records of the local police department. Only 19.8 percent of the total sample, including the high, medium, and low violators on the self-reporting schedule, was recorded in the police files.[6]

It seems clear that adequate inference in regard to the extent of juvenile delinquency in the United States cannot be made from either police records or juvenile court records. Hence, persons interested in prevention of delinquency must operate on the basis that the majority of instances of deviant behavior do not come to the attention of the social-control agents of society.

WHEN IS AND WHAT IS PREVENTION

In view of the very limited number of cases that do come to the attention of the authorities, the question becomes, At what point in the age of a young person and at what point in unreported involvement should prevention be inaugurated? Clearly, intervention needs to occur before too much unreported delinquency takes place in the life of a youth. The ideal, of course, would be to introduce prevention before a child's first serious delinquent act took place.

The time period in the lives of preadolescent children when fairly serious deviations take place is also not a consistent factor. Several authorities in the United States hold the opinion that it is possible to develop methods to screen children in order to determine at what point in time they are likely to turn toward deviance. One important piece of research, which compared a sample of delinquent and officially nondelinquent boys in Boston, indicated that the boy most likely to become involved in delinquency characteristically would be mesomorphic (muscular), aggressive, hostile and defiant, a direct (discrete) learner, and from a bad home situation.[7] Other authorities, such as Kvaraceus, developed evidence to show that teachers as well as other trained workers in contact with youth can make good prognostications as to which of the boys who had come to their attention were headed for delinquency.[8] As a matter of fact, one of the most important early prevention projects had teachers and social workers screen boys under 12 years of age for those who were and were not headed for trouble. This project, which is mentioned in the next chapter, did intensive counseling work with a split half (that is, randomly selected groups of experimentals and controls) of the youths who were prognosticated as headed for delinquency.[9] In fact, the present project of the authors also obtained teacher prognostications on sixth-grade boys in the inner city, as the basis for working with those who were headed for trouble with the law.

Undoubtedly, the earlier in life youths are reached for prevention, the better the focus—certainly by 12 years of age or earlier. In addition, if selection of subjects can be made on a feasible basis, so much the better. But just how much unreported involvement would have to take place before prevention efforts reach a selected sample of youths, we cannot know. Probably, the amount of involvement should not be serious enough in quantity and quality to bring the youth to the attention of the police. If an effective decision can be made as to which youths should be reached and at what point in their gravitation toward delinquency, then the next matter to be considered is how and with what means the program should reach them.

1. "Crime in the United States," *Uniform Crime Reports, 1970* (Washington, D.C.: Federal Bureau of Investigation, August 31, 1971), p. 128, table 29.

2. Ibid., p. 130, table 31.

3. *Juvenile Court Statistics, 1969* (Washington, D.C.: U.S. Department of Health, Education, and Welfare), p. 7, table 1.

4. *Statistics of Public Institutions for Delinquent Children, 1970* (Washington, D.C.: U.S. Department of Health, Education, and Welfare, June 30, 1971), p. 5.

5. See Austin L. Porterfield, *Youth in Trouble* (Fort Worth, Tex.: Leo Potisham Foundation, 1946); and F. Ivan Nye and James F. Short, Jr., "Scaling Delinquent Behavior," *American Sociological Review* 22 (June 1957):326–31.

6. Robert H. Hardt, "Delinquency and Social Class: Studies of Juvenile Deviations or Police Dispositions," Youth Development Center, Syracuse University, December 15, 1964, mimeographed, pp. 2–3, 7. See also Robert H. Hardt and Sandra J. Peterson, "Arrests of Self and Friends as Indicators of Delinquency Involvement," *Journal of Research in Crime and Delinquency* 5, no. 1, (January 1968):44–51.

7. Sheldon and Eleanor Glueck, *Unravelling Juvenile Delinquency* (Cambridge, Mass.: Harvard University Press, 1950), pp. 281–82.

8. See William C. Kvaraceus, *K D Proneness Check List* (New York: World Book Company, 1953).

9. P. S. deQ Cabot, "A Long-Term Study of Children: The Cambridge-Somerville Youth Study," *Child Development* 2, no. 2, (1950):143–49.

CHAPTER THREE

A Review of Delinquency Prevention Programs

It would be fair and accurate to say that the United States has tried harder than any other country in the world to implement two types of programs for the prevention of juvenile delinquency. Both have been well intentioned but operationally ineffective.

The growth of settlement houses in the slum areas of large American cities attempted to reach youths as well as adults; but, until rather recently, these neighborhood houses attracted boys and girls who, although living in the slums, were not so likely to get into trouble with the law. The local youths who were headed for trouble were seldom reached by the settlement house or its programs. In some instances, they were even asked not to participate. When city parks and playgrounds were developed in the United States, their programs attracted the so-called good kids, not the bad ones. The latter were frequently told to get out and stay away.

Likewise, when the Boy Scouts, the YMCA, and the

Boys' Clubs developed, prior to World War I, their programs did not attract the delinquent boy. It was the nondelinquent boy who saw merit in these early programs and was, consequently, attracted to them. Even as late as the 1920s, Thrasher found from firsthand research that a boys' club in New York City had difficulty in holding on to its members, that no conscious attempt was made to reach the potential delinquent, and that the program had no influence in decreasing the offenses committed by its members.[1]

Presumably, the school programs focusing on reduction of truancy, which was conceived to be the first step toward official delinquency, have had a limited effect on prevention of delinquency involvement, even when they substituted the use of "visiting teacher" for truant officer.

With the advent of clinical psychiatry and psychology, especially after Dr. William Healy's demonstrations of the use of clinics for the diagnosis and treatment of delinquent and problem children, several child guidance clinics were developed in the large cities of the United States. But their treatment options and modalities were very limited. Not only were they very costly to operate on a per case basis but they had a very small and most insignificant intake. Obviously, the reaching power of the pre–World War II delinquency prevention programs was very, very limited.

Perhaps the first demonstration that attempted to get on target was made by Clifford R. Shaw in Chicago beginning in the early thirties.[2] Shaw tried to reach the boys in the gangs of the high-delinquency areas of Chicago, and he developed a technique for training an indigenous young adult male known to, and accepted by, the boys to act as group leader to an assigned gang. The problem here was for the leader to find ways of diverting behavior of the group from delinquency involvement to interesting nondelinquent activities.

The program of the so-called detached worker,[3] which was developed by the New York City Youth Board in the late forties, was an extension of Shaw's approach. The worker, who could be accepted by the local boys, was sent to the street corner. It was not expected that the street-corner gang would come to the playground, the YMCA, the Boys' Club, or the settlement house. A more recent (ca. 1961) demonstration of reaching the gang was made by the Chicago Youth Development Project, in which three Boys' Clubs of Chicago attempted to reach the "unreached" by so-called extension workers.[4]

In recent years, a limited number of gigantic prevention programs were established mainly in high-delinquency areas of large cities (ca. 1961), funded in part by President Kennedy's Committee on Juvenile Delinquency and Youth Crime. These programs were essentially "community based," and they represented a herculean effort to get local citizens involved in their own behalf and in providing services to overcome limited opportunity.

These large community-based programs were developed in the Lower East Side of Manhattan and in Harlem in New York City; in Boston; in New Haven; in Syracuse; in Los Angeles, and in Appalachia (Kanawah County, West Virginia).[5] All of these programs were supposed to have a built-in provision for evaluation of results, but, because of so many intervening variables, it is most difficult to assess whether these programs have had any discernible preventive effect.

A PIONEERING EXPERIMENTAL DESIGN

One program in particular for prevention of delinquency had a built-in experimental design and should be mentioned. It was the Cambridge-Somerville Youth Study,[6] which was established in 1935 in the two contiguous communities that make up Greater Boston. The main objective was to discover whether close contact with so-called counselors could keep vulnerable 12-year-old boys from becoming delinquent. The project ran into difficulties of execution during the war years and was never completed as planned. Nevertheless, the experimental design was outstanding.

The Cambridge-Somerville project asked teachers, social workers, and staff members of the juvenile court to nominate boys under 12 years of age who could profit from guidance by counselors. They were asked to submit names of boys who were "difficult" as well as boys who were "average" in behavior development. The names of 1,900 boys were submitted, and out of this list 325 matched pairs (650 boys) were chosen as candidates for the project. By random selection, one boy of a matched pair was placed in the treatment group (receiving guidance), and the other boy was not given guidance (only follow-up).

In addition to the experimental design, the Cambridge-Somerville project had certain other important dimensions that should be indicated. It attempted not only to reach boys showing vulnerability toward delinquency but also to start with the "treatment" boy in late childhood or at the threshold of adolescence, when boys begin gravitating toward peer groups and gangs where the companionship factor in delinquency is most visibly operable.

THE DESIGN OF A RECENT EXPERIMENT

A very recent experimental project, entitled "Effectiveness of Social Work with Acting-Out Youth," was developed at the Seattle Atlantic Street Center in Seattle, Washington. Actually, this inner-city settlement house, after fifty years of operation, decided in 1959 to specialize in working with maladjusted youth. In 1962, the Center generated an experimental program to test the effectiveness of intensive social-work contact with "acting-out" boys. Approximately the first two and one-half years were devoted to preparation and pretesting. During the next two years the so-called experimental group of high-risk boys received the intensive casework treatment. An evaluation of the boys was made during the last six months of the fifth year. The sixth and seventh years were devoted entirely to follow-up evaluation.

One hundred and twenty-seven boys from the seventh grades of two inner-city junior high schools were selected by various measures as being boys of high risk for delinquency from among the total number of seventh-grade boys in these two schools. Fifty-four of the 127 were randomly chosen as subjects for the project (the experimental boys) ; 18, as stand-by experimentals in the event of dropout; and 44, as control subjects (not entered in the intensive-casework program). One of the original sample was eliminated because of an error in the selection process.

The 54 experimental boys (finally reduced to 51 in the course of time) were assigned to three professionally trained male social workers; hence, each social worker had a case load of approximately 18 experimental boys. All of the 54 experimentals volunteered to participate in the program. A major part of the program consisted of weekly group sessions at the Center, involving recreation, discussion, and refreshments. The social workers maintained close contact with each boy at home, in his neighborhood, and at school, and also with the boy's family, teachers, and peer-group associates. The intensive service of the social worker was guided by five generalized goals: (1) confrontation (forcing the client and his family to recognize their problems); (2) support (bolstering the ego, intervention in behalf of the client, and so forth); (3) reality orientation (unwinding the denial and defense mechanisms); (4) social-psychological development (better understanding of relationships and of the motivations in back of behavior), and (5) ego identity (the development of a positive identity).[7]

EVOLUTION OF THE PRESENT PROJECT

The present demonstration project in delinquency prevention, located in the seventh grade of eight junior high schools of the inner city in Columbus, Ohio, evolved out of research that we had been doing for several years. Beginning in 1955,[8] we attempted to make soundings in the high-delinquency areas of Columbus relative to differences between sixth-grade boys (threshold age for ordinary delinquency) who were apparently *headed toward* and *not headed toward* delinquency. The sixth-grade teachers in sample elementary schools of the high-delinquency areas were asked to nominate the boys in their classes who, in their judgment, were likely to stay out of trouble with the law and likely also to finish high school. The investigators started with the nominated "good boys."

Two interviewers were sent to the home of each nominated "good boy" to contact the boy and his mother simultaneously (in separate rooms of their home). The interview was structured by use of a schedule that attempted to get at the boy's own view of himself and his outlook on life. The mother's schedule attempted to reveal the way she thought her son looked upon life and himself.

The following year (1956), the investigators returned to the same sixth-grade rooms and asked the teachers to nominate the boys in their classes who, in their judgment, were likely to get into trouble with the law (become delinquent) and were likely *not* to finish school. The same interview contacts were made with these boys and their mothers.

The investigators at the time were impressed with the difference between the so-called good boys and the so-called bad boys in regard to their outlook. The investigators called this outlook the self-concept. The nominated good boys seemingly had a favorable self-concept, whereas the nominated bad boys had an unfavorable one. The investigators at the time were also impressed with the possibility that a good self-concept might represent a sort of social-psychological vaccination against delinquency, whereas a poor self-concept might represent vulnerability toward delinquency. Furthermore, it appeared to the researchers that the good boy had, among other things working in his favor, an inner containment,[9] which helped him to steer himself in a nondelinquent direction in neighborhoods of high delinquency. The boys with a poor self-concept lacked an inner containing factor and were thus more susceptible to the pressures and pulls of life in the inner city. The investigators felt they were on the track of an important self factor[10] that might help to explain why some boys—probably the large majority —are able to steer away from delinquency involvement and some gravitate toward involvement. Subsequent research in Columbus, in Akron, and in Brooklyn gave considerable validation to the reality of a differential self-concept.

The Columbus school system's assistant superintendent in charge of instruction, who had been very cooperative in helping the investigators to expedite their initial research on the differential self-concept of the inner-city's nominated good and bad sixth-grade (12-year-old) boys, suggested that an actual application be made. The investigators designed a pilot project for the vulnerable sixth-grade boys in two classes of one elementary school in a high-delinquency area. The boys were selected by teacher nomination and were also screened for directionality toward delinquency by their responses to self-concept items and to the Socialization Scale of the California Psychological Inventory. In the first demonstration during the second semester of the 1959–60 school year, 12 sixth-grade boys in one elementary school were taken during the last hour of the school day into a special meeting place in the school and placed under the supervision of a graduate assistant who had been trained to present to the boys appropriate insights into life situations and appropriate "role models."

The pilot project was continued at the same school during the school year 1960–61. It was expanded in 1961–62 to four elementary schools in high-delinquency areas of Columbus. The results of this attempt to "beef up" the self by presentation of appropriate role models and by internalization of better self-concepts were encouraging, and the question arose whether it was possible to extend the project throughout the greater part of Columbus's inner city.

CHARACTERISTICS OF THE PROJECT

We finally decided that the best place in the Columbus school system to implement a demonstration-evaluation project was in the seventh grades of eight junior high schools that serve children in the high-delinquency areas. At this time, the seventh grades in the junior high schools of Columbus were operating so-called self-contained classes, in which pupils had the same teacher for three consecutive class periods of 40 minutes each (120 minutes) every school day during the entire year. The principal subjects usually covered in the self-contained classes were social studies, world geography, and English. Social studies consisted primarily of the study of Ohio history (required by law) as well as of state and local government.

The self-contained classes afforded the opportunity to infuse materials that could present models of behavior (principally role models) along with the required material. One self-contained class in each of the eight junior high schools was designated as the experimental class, in which role models would supplement the regular educational material. This designated class became an "all-boy" class, composed of randomly selected boys nominated as headed for trouble and not likely to finish school by their sixth-grade teachers and by the principals of the 44 feeder elementary schools. The project designated these boys as the "bad-boy experimentals." The remainder of the nominated so-called bad boys were assigned to the regular self-contained classes in the seventh grade, which included girls as well as the so-called good boys (designated by the teachers and principals as unlikely to get into trouble and likely to finish school). The regular self-contained seventh-grade classes did not receive the role-model and other supplementation, which was the medicine administered to "beef up" the self and thus to guide the youth away from delinquency involvement.

It will become apparent from the details in the next chapter that the project attempted to follow an experimental design: random assignment of the bad boys to the so-called treatment group and to the control group (not receiving the role-model medicine but only the regular diet), plus the assignment of the so-called good boys to a regular seventh-grade self-contained classroom. Thus, the project attempted to have an experimental group and a control group of boys headed toward delinquency plus a comparison group composed of boys supposedly moving in the positive direction of social adjustment.

At this juncture, if the characteristics of the Columbus delinquency prevention program need to be summarized, the following points can be noted.

1. The project operated in high-delinquency areas.
2. The attempt was made to reach the boys headed for delinquency involvement.
3. The boys were still at threshold age for delinquency (13 years of age and in the seventh grade).
4. The classroom and the teacher were the educational vehicles of the program.
5. The guiding principle of the program was the

presentation of an educational supplement to a treatment group that attempted to get the youth to internalize better models of behavior and thus strengthen the steering power of his self.

6. The program presented one academic year's exposure of the treatment group in an all-boy class to the role model supplement infused into the regular school fare.

7. The project utilized an experimental design to facilitate the testing of outcome.

1. Frederick M. Thrasher, "The Boys' Club and Juvenile Delinquency," *American Journal of Sociology* 42 (July 1936):67–68.

2. Solomon Kobrin, "The Chicago Area Project—A 25-Year Assessment," *Annals of the American Academy of Political and Social Science* 32 (March 1959):22–28.

3. Ralph W. Whelan, "New York City Serves Its Youth: A Report on the Work of the Youth Board," mimeographed (New York: New York City Youth Board, 1956). See also Walter B. Miller, "Preventive Work with Street-Corner Groups: Boston Delinquency Project," *Annals of the American Academy of Political and Social Science* 32 (March 1959) : 98–106.

4. Hans W. Mattick and Nathan S. Caplan, "The Chicago Youth Development Project," mimeographed (Chicago: Chicago Boys' Club, 304 W. Randolph Street, April 1, 1962), pp. 1, 2, 10, 11, 18–20, 22, 25, 26, 29–39.

5. President's Committee on Delinquency and Youth Crime, "Counter-Attack on Delinquency," mimeographed (Washington, 1965).

6. Edwin Powers and Helen Witmer, *An Experiment in Prevention of Delinquency: The Cambridge-Somerville Youth Study* (New York: Columbia University Press, 1951), pp. 324–36. Joan and William McCord, "A Follow-Up Report on the Cambridge-Somerville Youth Study," *Annals of the American Academy of Political and Social Science* 32 (March 1959) : 96.

7. James R. Seaberg, "An Example of Social Work Intervention with Acting-Out Youth," (Seattle, Wash.: Seattle Atlantic Street Center, 2103 S. Atlantic Street, 98144).

8. Walter C. Reckless, Simon Dinitz, and Ellen Murray, "The 'Good' Boy in a High Delinquency Area," *Journal of Criminal Law,*

Criminology and Police Science 48 (August 1957) :17–25. Walter C. Reckless, Simon Dinitz, and Ellen Murray, "Self Component as an Insulator Against Delinquency," *American Sociological Review* 21 (December 1956) :221–23. Walter C. Reckless, Simon Dinitz, and Barbara Kay, "The Self Component in Potential Delinquency," *American Sociological Review* 22 (October 1957) :566–70. Simon Dinitz and Barbara Kay, "Group Gradients in Delinquency Potential and Achievement Scores of Sixth Graders," *Journal of Orthopsychiatry* 28 (July 1958) :598–606. Simon Dinitz, Frank R. Scarpitti, and Walter C. Reckless, "Delinquency Vulnerability: A Cross Group and Longitudinal Analysis," *American Sociological Review* 27, no. 4 (August 1962) :517. Ernest P. Donald, "Self Concept of Sixth-Grade Boys: A Study of Delinquency Proneness" (Ph.D. diss., Ohio State University, 1963). See also Ernest P. Donald and Simon Dinitz, "Self Concept and Delinquency Proneness," in *Interdisciplinary Problems in Criminology: Papers of the American Society of Criminology, 1964*, ed. Walter C. Reckless and Charles L. Newman (Columbus: Ohio State University, College of Commerce and Administration, 1965), pp. 49–59.

9. Walter C. Reckless, *The Crime Problem*, 4th ed. (New York: Appleton-Century-Crofts, 1967), pp. 475–78.

10. Ibid., pp. 444, 467–68.

CHAPTER FOUR

Project Design

The project attempted to follow an experimental design to determine whether potentially delinquent and potentially drop-out boys who are given a year's intervention in the seventh grade will have a lower rate of delinquency incidence in a four-year follow-up period than the untreated group of potential delinquents and potential drop-outs.

SELECTION OF THE SAMPLE

As has been indicated briefly, the investigators asked teachers and principals in 44 elementary schools in the inner city in Columbus, Ohio, to evaluate all of their male sixth-grade students as candidates for delinquency status using three categories: (a) *unlikely*, (b) *possible*, and (c) *likely*. "Good" boys obviously constituted the first category, "vulnerable" or "bad" boys the last two.

Teachers and principals were also asked to indicate the likelihood of each sixth-grade boy's finishing high school. The previous experience of the investigators with sixth-grade-teacher ratings indicated that such ratings were quite realistic. In other words, the sixth-grade teacher, who had the boy in class the whole school day for the entire school year, had become well acquainted with his development and was, therefore, likely to be a fair prognosticator of his outcome.

The sixth-grade teacher's rating list was reviewed by the principal in each elementary school. He usually confirmed the rating, not just as a procedural confirmation but as an actual one based on his knowledge of the boy. Differences between the ratings of principal and teacher appeared in only a very few instances (see table 3, chapter 5).

Beginning with the second cohort, the investigators asked the sixth-grade teachers to indicate those boys on their class lists with IQ test results lower than 70 as well as the boys who showed obvious emotional disturbances and serious physical handicaps. These boys were eliminated from the samples in the second and third cohort years.

The rating lists of the sixth-grade teachers were turned over to the staff of the project. The co-principal investigator and the project director made random assignments of the vulnerable boys who were to be placed in the all-boy experimental self-contained seventh-grade classes, of the vulnerable boys who were to be placed in the regular self-contained seventh-grade classes, and of the good boys (not headed for trouble) who were to be assigned to the regular self-contained classes and followed as a special comparison group.

These random assignments were made from cards

with name identification, obtained from the sixth-grade teachers. However, because of class sizes of the elementary schools that fed the junior high schools and the requirement in the eight junior high schools to assign as close to 35 boys as possible to the experimental classes, it was necessary to assign randomly almost two-thirds of the vulnerable boys to the experimental classes. It was only possible to approximate a 50–50 split of the bad boys (*likely* or *possible* to become involved in law-violating activity) in the third cohort year (1965–66).

PROJECT TEACHERS AND STAFF

It was decided to select the project teachers for the experimental self-contained classes from the male teachers who ordinarily taught self-contained classes in the seventh grade. The assistant superintendent in charge of instruction of the Columbus public schools suggested several male seventh-grade teachers who might well qualify for the task. The principal investigator, after looking over the credentials and after a personal interview with each prospect, made the selection of the four male teachers who became the project teachers.

The four selectees were gathered in a training seminar at the Ohio State University with the principal investigator for a two-week period during July 1963. Discussion was held on topics pertinent to the project and pertinent to the understanding of the particular boys on whom the experimental classes would focus. Suggestions for effective topics and methods of presentation as well as approaches to the behavior problems of the boys and their level of comprehension were discussed. One of the main results of the daily seminar was the development of a close identification—a sort of "in-group feeling." The selected project teachers were paid a modest salary for the overtime spent in the training seminar during the vacation season. The director of the project joined the staff in late August 1963. The secretary and the research assistant of the project were also selected and integrated at this time. The consulting psychiatrist also held a preliminary session with the four project teachers and the director. When school opened, the project was ready to go.

ASSIGNMENT OF CASES

Arrangements were made with the principals of each of the eight junior high schools to place the incoming seventh-grade boys according to assignments decided upon by the project staff. Case folders were prepared for each boy assigned to the experimental class, to a regular class, and also for the sample of the good-boy comparisons who also received the regular seventh-grade self-contained class curriculum.

The same assignment procedure was followed in September of three consecutive school years beginning in 1963, 1964, and 1965. Consequently, the project had three yearly cohorts and three subgroups in each yearly cohort: the randomly selected bad boys who were assigned to the all-boy experimental self-contained class; the bad boys who were assigned to the control group, receiving the regular material of the self-contained class; and a randomly selected sample (about 15 percent) of the good boys who were also assigned to a regular self-contained class.

INTERPRETATION OF THE EXPERIMENTAL CLASS

It was agreed between the project teachers, the staff, and the principals that inquiries from boys as to why they were assigned to the experimental class would be answered by the following statement: "Mr. Jones wanted to have an all-boy class, and he picked you." This seemed to allay the suspicions of the experimental boys and certainly answered the questions, "Why are we here? Are we 'hoods'?"

During the first part of the demonstration, the project director visited each junior high school at a teachers' assembly or meeting and presented a statement of the design and purpose of the project and the experimental class. This did much to improve understanding and to further cooperation.

ASSIGNMENT OF PROJECT TEACHERS

By arrangement with the Columbus school authorities, including the principals of the junior high schools, each of the four project teachers was assigned to handle the experimental all-boy self-contained class in two junior high schools. He handled the all-boy experimental class in one junior high school in the morning and in another in the afternoon. The staff made certain that each project teacher was able to identify with each of his two junior high schools, so as not to be considered a part-time outsider. The morning assignment consisted of conducting the all-boy experimental self-contained class for three class periods (120 minutes) plus other teaching duties that were assigned at that particular junior high school. The afternoon assignment in a different school duplicated the morning assignment.

DAILY AFTER-SCHOOL SESSIONS

The four project teachers reported each school-day afternoon to the project director for an approximate two-hour discussion session. The project teachers received an overtime stipend for this after-school-hours assignment. At these daily sessions, difficulties were presented and problems solved. Proposals for presentation of role-model and related materials were discussed, and agreements were reached on what content to present and in what form. In other words, lesson plans were produced. Agreement was also reached as to when (on what day) a particular lesson plan was to be offered in each experimental self-contained class. The supplemental curriculum content consisting of the role-model lesson plans was a product of these daily after-school sessions, particularly in the first year of the project.

DISCUSSIONS SESSIONS WITH THE STAFF PSYCHIATRIST

Each Saturday, excluding holidays, was devoted to a two-hour morning session with the project's consulting psychiatrist attended by the project director and the four project teachers. Discussions were focused on the behavioral problems that arose in the experimental self-contained classes, and suggestions were developed as to how to handle these problems in the classroom and how to approach the special problems of individual boys.

CLASSROOM DISCIPLINE

In particular, a plan of classroom conduct regulation was developed in the initial Saturday session. This was called, in the words of the consulting psychiatrist, "respecting the rights of others."[1] According to this plan, a boy in any of the eight experimental classes whose behavior was disturbing or rule-violating was asked to leave the group and to sit in front of the classroom door until he felt he was ready to join the class again and to "respect the rights of others." Under this plan, no boy was sent to the principal's office for misconduct. The project teachers and the staff of the project were convinced that the "mutual respect" approach to classroom discipline worked very successfully, that it enhanced learning on the part of the pupils, and that it increased the effectiveness of the teachers.

SECOND AND THIRD YEARS

Most of the decisions on the content and the form of presentation of models of behavior (lesson plans) were made the first year by the project teachers and the staff of the project. However, the lesson plans were improved in content and presentation during the second year in the daily after-school sessions. During the third year, the afternoons of the project teachers were in large part devoted to home calls on the families of the individual boys in the project classes. This was looked upon as adding an extra reinforcement to the content of the role-model supplement of the self-contained classes.

REMEDIAL READING

Very early in the first year of the project, the teachers and the staff became increasingly concerned with the fact that the experimental boys were behind in reading ability. They averaged 1.05 years below grade level. At the end of the sixth-grade, they ranged in reading achievement level all the way from 2.6 to 10.1 grade level. (The IQ averaged 93.96 and ranged from 65 to 140.)[2] During the first year, the project purchased an ample supply of paperback novels, biographies, and histories, which were placed in the classroom library and made readily available to the boys in the experimental class. The two most popular books were found to be H. G. Wells's *The Time Machine* and Don K. Stanford's *The Red Car*. These two books were adopted as texts, and exercises were developed covering various pages.[3]

After examining many workbooks, the staff discovered that the *Turner-Livingston Reading Series* dealt with topics closely paralleling the project's five curriculum topics for role-model building, and the series was adopted. The staff also used a third set of remedial reading materials from the *Reader's Digest Reading Skill Builder Series*.[4]

A series of "shotgun" exercises that focused on nearly every type of reading problem was developed during the second year of the project. Each project teacher was given a set of exercises and a handbook with instructions on how to teach the particular principle involved. When he discovered a commonly shared reading difficulty in his class, he pulled the appropriate exercise from the file and did remedial work then and there.[5] The experimental classes, beginning in the second cohort year (1964–65) devoted four 40-minute periods per week to this remedial reading program. One final resource was used: the experimental classes received copies of the morning newspaper twice a week. The pupils read orally or silently news items of interest to them and then discussed the contents.

CONTENT OF THE ROLE-MODEL SUPPLEMENT

In addition to the project teacher's approximating the role of a "significant other" in the lives of the experimental boys, the interaction of an all-boy class, the measures taken to improve reading, and the development of a special classroom discipline system (respecting the rights of others), the main thrust of the experimental program consisted of the presentation of role-model material to the pupils. This material became a supplement to the normally taught English, world geography, and social studies in the self-contained classes of the Columbus public school system's seventh grades.

The director of the project and the project teachers agreed on the general topics to be contained in the role-model supplement. There were five main topics: (1) The World of Work; (2) The School and You; (3) The House We Live In (a presentation of government services); (4) Getting Along with Others; and (5) The Family. The lesson plans that were generated under each topic were presented in this sequence during the school year.[6]

Appendix A presents the Curriculum Calendar for each of the five main topics. It should be noted that adjustments for rotation of films and other presentations had to be made among the four project teachers, so that Mr. A would show the film to his two experimental classes on one day; Mr. B., the next day; Mr. C., next; and Mr. D., next. A sample lesson plan for each of the five topics is duplicated in Appendix B. In reading the sample lesson plans, particular attention should be paid to the implications for communicating role models without "preaching" to the boys about the do's and the don'ts of American society.

UNIFORM DELAYED INTRODUCTION OF THE LESSON PLANS

It was definitely agreed by the staff and the project teachers that the lesson plans in the experimental all-boy seventh-grade self-contained class in each of the eight junior high schools would not be introduced until the fourth week of the new fall term. The reason for the delay in each cohort year was to prevent any initial suspicions, on the part of the experimental boys as well as the boys and girls in the regular self-contained classes, that the all-boy class was something special, unusual, or off-beat. The delay also gave the project teacher time to legitimize and justify the all-boy class before comparisons and criticisms could be made relative to the curriculum offerings in the regular self-contained classes. The uniqueness of the all-boy class had time to diminish before the special lesson plans were introduced.

DATA INPUT AND EVALUATION

A case folder was kept on each vulnerable boy as-signed to the experimental class as well as on each vulnerable boy assigned to the regular self-contained classes (constituting the control group) and on each so-called good-boy comparison also assigned to the regular self-contained classes in the eight junior high schools. Information obtained on each boy, beginning with the ratings by the sixth-grade teachers, was kept and filed in his folder. Subsequent school clearances regarding attendance information, conduct reports, and school performance were obtained in June of each year. The police clearance, indicating which boys had been referred to, or arrested by, the police, was made in August of each year. The clearances, of course, were made by name for each member of the 1963, 1964, and 1965 cohorts, but were classified by case-folder information as experimentals, bad-boy controls, and good-boy comparisons.

In addition to the initial case information and the school and police clearances, the staff administered certain pre- and post-tests. The first cohort of boys was administered a battery of tests while still in the sixth-grade, which included selected items from the Socialization Scale of the California Psychological Inventory, from the significant self-concept items developed previously by the investigators, and from Rothstein's interpersonal-competence items. In May, toward the end of the first cohort year, the same battery of tests was administered to the boys.

It was found that the battery of tests used the first year was not satisfactory for measuring possible change in direction of behavior or in outlook.[7] Consequently, the staff developed a different battery of tests that would be more sensitive to the kinds of changes the project was trying to produce in the experimental boys. These tests were to be administered at the beginning and at the end of the school year (referred to hereafter as pre-test and post-test). An instrument was developed and pretested that, according to Guttman's method of scaling, had 6 subscales dealing with the boy's outlook on school and teachers[8] and 9 subscales dealing with the boy's outlook on the law, the courts, the police, and probation officers.[9] These two sets of Guttman subscales were used for the last two cohorts

(1964–65 and 1965–66) as pre-tests at the beginning of the school year and as post-tests at the end of the school year. In addition, the second and third cohorts were also administered (at the beginning and end of the school year) a value orientation instrument[10] that attempted to measure the extent to which a youth subscribed to certain social values.

As a special input into the data bank of the project, the investigators and the director decided to make a follow-up study of the experimental and the bad-boy controls in the second cohort (1964–65) in the spring of 1967, which was two years after the school year that contained the role-model supplement for the boys assigned to the experimental all-boy self-contained class. This particular follow-up information consisted of a structured interview of the boy by the former project teacher and of an inventory of self-reporting items (filled out by the boy) relative to how often he had done certain things. The results of this special study form a special section of this report (see chapter 8).

1. W. Hugh Missildine, "The Mutual Respect Approach to Child Guidance: A Report of 97 Cases from Private Practice," *American Journal of Diseases of Children* 104 (August 1962) :116–21.

2. Nason E. Hall and Gordon P. Waldo, "Remedial Reading for the Disadvantaged," *Journal of Reading* 11, no. 2 (November 1967) :81.

3. Ibid., p. 82.

4. Ibid., p. 83.

5. Ibid.

6. Nason E. Hall et al, *Youth Development Project: Curriculum Guide, Lesson Plans, and Supplementary Materials* (Columbus: Ohio State University Research Foundation, 1964).

7. Margaret Ann Zahn, "An Evaluation of an Experimental Delinquency Prevention Program" (Masters thesis, Ohio State University, 1964), pp. 45, 46, 65–69.

8. Nason E. Hall and Gordon P. Waldo, "School Identification and Delinquency Proneness," *Journal of Research in Crime and Delinquency* 4, no. 2 (July 1967):234–35.

9. Gordon P. Waldo, "Boys' Perceptions of Outer Containment and Delinquency Potential," (Ph.D. diss., Ohio State University, 1967), pp. 46–48, 81–106, 124–25, 154–71.

10. Judson R. Landis and Frank R. Scarpitti, "Delinquent and Non-Delinquent Value Orientation and Opportunity Awareness," in *Interdisciplinary Problems in Criminology: Papers of the American Society of Criminology, 1964,* ed. Walter C. Reckless and Charles L. Newman (Columbus: Ohio State University, College of Commerce and Administration, 1965), pp. 67–68 (value-orientation items).

CHAPTER FIVE

The Characteristics
of the Project Boys

In the three years of the demonstration project, 1,726 boys were studied—507 the first year, 544 the second year, and 675 the third year. Table 1 indicates the distribution of these pupils in the three cohort years.

There was, it will be noted, a considerable increase in the number of boys taken into the program in the last year of the demonstration. This increase occurred chiefly in the pool of boys nominated by their teachers as potentially delinquent (that is, nominated as *likely* or *possible* candidates) and assigned to the control group. In explaining this addition of over 100 boys in the third year, two factors need to be mentioned. First, and clearly foremost, the project staff worked diligently to obtain a complete set of teacher nominations. At least two team members visited each of the 44 elementary feeder schools in an effort to reduce the loss of unnominated cases. The effects of these continuing public-relations efforts were clearly evident as the number of experimental and control boys increased in the second and especially in the third years. In addition, a ninth inner-city junior high school opened just prior to the third year of the demonstration. Nominated boys who normally would have gone to other schools were now sent here, making them eligible as controls. This new inner-city school alone added an additional 43 boys to the project.

Overall, experimental subjects constituted 36.6% of all subjects, and 39.6%, 40.3%, and 31.4%, respectively, of the pupils in the three years. The controls accounted for 26.8% of all subjects and 22.7%, 22.6%, and 33.2% of the boys in the 1963, 1964, and 1965 cohorts, respectively. Good-boy comparisons constituted 36.6% of all 1,726 boys and 37.7%, 37.1%, and 35.4%, respectively, of the total number of pupils in each of the three years (see table 1).

TABLE 1

NUMBER AND PERCENTAGE OF EXPERIMENTAL, CONTROL, AND COMPARISON BOYS IN THE THREE COHORT YEARS

	1963–64		1964–65		1965–66		TOTAL	
	N	%	N	%	N	%	N	%
Experimentals.......	201	39.6	219	40.3	212	31.4	632	36.6
Controls...........	115	22.7	123	22.6	224	33.2	462	26.8
Comparisons........	191	37.7	202	37.1	239	35.4	632	36.6
Total...........	507	100.0	544	100.0	675	100.0	1,726	100.0

TEACHER NOMINATIONS

In the initial cohort selected in 1963–64, as noted previously, teachers and principals jointly evaluated all of their male sixth-grade students as (a) *likely* to get into difficulty with the law, (b) *possible*, and (c) *unlikely* to get into trouble. Of the 316 boys who eventually were randomly assigned to the experimental or control groups, 83 were nominated for the *likely* group; the teachers and principals placed the remaining 233 boys in the *possible* category (see table 2).

TABLE 2

NUMBER AND PERCENTAGE OF ASSIGNMENT OF SUBJECTS IN THE FIRST COHORT, ACCORDING TO TEACHER-PRINCIPAL NOMINATION, 1963–64

ASSIGNMENT	UNLIKELY		POSSIBLE		LIKELY		TOTAL	
	N	%	N	%	N	%	N	%
Experimentals....	...	...	152	75.6	49	24.4	201	39.6
Controls.........	...	...	81	70.4	34	29.6	115	22.7
Comparisons.....	191	100.0	...	...	...	...	191	37.7
Total.........	191	37.6	233	45.9	83	16.5	507	100.0

In the second year of student intake into the program, the nominating procedure was somewhat refined, so that teachers and principals independently of each other evaluated all the boys. Of the 342 experimental and control boys, 46 (13.5%) were nominated as *unlikely* by their teachers but as *possible* or *likely* by the principals; 16 more (4.7%) were listed as *possible* by the teachers but as *unlikely* by the principals. The majority, 204 (59.6%) were listed as *possible* by the teachers and as either *possible* or *likely* by the principals. One boy, on the other hand, was thought *likely* by his teacher but not by the principal; and 75 (21.9%) were rated as *likely* by their teachers and as *likely* or *possible* by the principals (see table 3).

Very much the same distribution of nominations occurred for the third cohort (1965–66). Of the 436 experimentals and controls, 46 (10.6%) were nominated as *unlikely* by the teachers but not by the principals; 37 (8.5%) as *possible* by the teachers but as *unlikely*

TABLE 3

NUMBER AND PERCENTAGE OF ASSIGNMENTS OF SUBJECTS IN THE SECOND COHORT, ACCORDING TO TEACHER AND PRINCIPAL NOMINATIONS, 1964–65

NOMINATIONS BY TEACHER	PRINCIPAL	EXPERIMENTALS N	%	CONTROLS N	%	COMPARISONS N	%	TOTAL	PERCENT
Unlikely	Unlikely	...	...	...	...	202	100.0	202	100.0
Unlikely	Possible	30	66.7	15	33.3	...	...	45	100.0
Unlikely	Likely	1	100.0	...	...	...	...	1	100.0
Possible	Unlikely	9	56.3	7	43.7	...	...	16	100.0
Possible	Possible	109	64.9	59	35.1	...	...	168	100.0
Possible	Likely	19	52.8	17	47.2	...	...	36	100.0
Likely	Unlikely	1	100.0	...	...	...	...	1	100.0
Likely	Possible	6	75.0	2	25.0	...	...	8	100.0
Likely	Likely	44	65.7	23	34.3	...	...	67	100.0
Total		219	40.3	123	22.6	202	37.1	544	100.0

by the principals; 237 (54.4%) as *possible* by the teachers and as *possible* or *likely* by the principals. Only two boys (0.5%) were classified as *likely* by the teachers and not by the principals, and 114 (26.1%) were rated as *likely* by the teachers and as *likely* or *possible* by the principals (see table 4).

It should be noted that in the two years 1964–65 and 1965–66, during which teachers and principals independently of one another rated their students, there were only 6 cases in which the teacher nominated boys as *unlikely* and the principals as *likely*. Conversely, there were only 3 boys in the two cohort years who were nominated as *likely* by the teachers and as *unlikely* by the principals.

SAMPLE CHARACTERISTICS

Age

The age distribution of the experimental, control, and comparison subjects in each of the three cohort years is displayed in summary table 5. It is evident from this table that, at intake to the study, the nominated bad boys, whether experimental or control, were about a half-year older on the average than the good-boy comparisons. The overall mean age of the experimentals was 13.25; of the controls 13.27; and of the good-boy comparisons, 12.76 years. This age differential reflects the generally poorer achievement of the nominated potential delinquents, which resulted in their being held back in school more often.

Race

The data indicate that about half of the experimental and control subjects were white, whereas a signifi-

TABLE 4

Number and Percentage of Assignments of Subjects in the Third Cohort,
According to Teacher and Principal Nominations, 1965–66

Nominations by Teacher	Principal	Experimentals		Controls		Comparisons		Total	Percent
		N	%	N	%	N	%		
Unlikely	Unlikely					239	100.0	239	100.0
Unlikely	Possible	20	48.8	21	51.2			41	100.0
Unlikely	Likely	2	40.0	3	60.0			5	100.0
Possible	Unlikely	17	45.5	20	54.5			37	100.0
Possible	Possible	93	46.5	107	53.5			200	100.0
Possible	Likely	20	54.5	17	45.5			37	100.0
Likely	Unlikely			2	100.0			2	100.0
Likely	Possible	13	56.5	10	43.5			23	100.0
Likely	Likely	47	51.6	44	48.4			91	100.0
Total		212	31.4	224	33.2	239	35.4	675	100.0

cantly greater percentage—over three-fifths of the good-boy comparisons were white (see table 5). There was only minor fluctuation in these percentages in the three intake years. (It should be noted that the race of the pupil was not on the cards from which students were randomly designated as either experimental or control subjects.)

The much higher percentage of blacks among the bad-boy nominees is hardly surprising. The difference has been attributed to the black-white disparities in income, occupation, life style, family disorganization, as well as in teacher sensitivity, expectations, and bias. In earlier research on teacher nominations of predelinquent boys, it was discovered that teacher evaluations are largely based on four clusters of variables: knowledge of the family situation of the boy, academic performance, personality attributes, and the degree of "acting out" in school that presented discipline problems.[1] On at least three of these variables, black boys are likely to fare more poorly than white boys. In addition, teachers are likely to expect greater delinquency potential in black boys. Likewise, the previous work of the investigators suggests that women teachers consistently nominate a higher percentage of boys as predelinquents than do male teachers. This occurs despite the policy of placing the more difficult boys in classes taught by males.

Family Status

As with age and race, the family status of the 1,726 pupils varied markedly by type of nomination. As seen in the section on family composition in table 5, 54.8% of the experimental boys, 56.1% of the controls, and

TABLE 5

CHARACTERISTICS OF 1,726 EXPERIMENTAL, CONTROL, AND COMPARISON BOYS IN THE THREE COHORTS

	1963–64			1964–65			1965–66			TOTAL		
	Experimental	Control	Comparison	Experimental	Control	Comparison	Experimental	Control	Comparison	Experimental	Control	Comparison
Demographic												
Mean age	13.3	13.3	12.9	13.3	13.3	12.7	13.3	13.3	12.7	13.2	13.3	12.8
Percent white	50.8	52.2	62.8	49.8	66.7	63.9	52.4	40.6	59.8	50.9	50.4	62.0
*Family composition**												
Intact	57.2	55.7	66.7	51.6	59.4	67.2	56.6	55.7	68.5	54.8	56.1	67.2
Female based	21.9	27.8	17.8	31.1	26.8	19.3	28.0	26.3	17.1	27.2	26.8	18.0
Surrogate	14.9	11.2	12.4	12.8	10.5	12.0	14.0	16.1	13.6	13.9	13.9	13.0
Other	6.0	5.3	3.1	4.5	3.3	1.5	1.4	1.9	0.8	4.1	3.2	1.8
Median socioeconomic status†												
All families	19	19	22	19	19	18	19	18	22	19	19	22
Male headed families	19	17	22	18	19	19	19	18	23	19	18	22
School achievement												
Mean IQ	89.9	88.0	96.7	92.8	93.1	100.9	92.4	90.0	102.9	91.6	90.3	100.4
Mean reading achievement	6.0	5.8	7.1	5.8	6.0	6.6	5.3	5.2	6.5	5.7	5.5	6.7
Mean arithmetic achievement	6.8	6.0	7.5	6.3	6.5	7.1	5.7	5.4	6.7	6.3	5.9	7.1
Mean grade point‡	3.3	3.3	2.7	3.3	3.4	2.5	3.3	3.4	2.5	3.3	3.4	2.5
School attendance§	.93	.93	.96	.94	.93	.96	.94	.94	.96	.94	.94	.96

* Given in column percentages.
† According to the Reiss system based on the occupational prestige of the breadwinner's job.
‡ A = 1, B = 2, C = 3, D = 4, and F = 5.
§ Percentage of days present out of the total number of school days.

67.2% of the good-boy comparisons came from intact families (both biological parents or both adoptive parents being present). Approximately 27% of nominated experimentals and controls as against 18% of the nominated good-boy comparisons were from female-based households (mother, grandmother, or aunt, alone, or in some combination of the three). Surrogate family arrangements (aunt and uncle, foster parents, and so forth) were found in about 13% of all three subgroups of boys (experimental, control, and comparison).

The family composition of the boys varied only slightly with year of intake into the program, but more boys came from female-based households in the second year of intake than in either the first or third years. Such random variation is to be anticipated and presents no special problems.

Social Class

All of the boys in the demonstration program were chosen from inner-city elementary schools. These 44 schools are located in the lowest socioeconomic quartile as measured by such standard census characteristics as median family income, median rental, median educational attainment, occupational distribution, adequacy of housing, and the average number of persons per room. Using the Albert Reiss socioeconomic classification system,[2] which is based on occupational rankings, the median class index score of the families of the experimentals and the controls was 19 in each case, and the index for the families of the good-boy comparisons stood at 21. Since most professionals and white-collar workers are ranked in the 70s, 80s, and 90s according to the Reiss system and since even the skilled workers are ranked in the 40s and 50s, it is apparent that the occupational index of the subjects' families reflects unskilled, service, and other low-prestige jobs.

It was originally assumed that the large number of female-based households, in which a woman was the breadwinner, accounted for these low socioeconomic index scores. For this reason, two analyses were run: one for the families with a male breadwinner present and the other for the families with no male breadwinner. The net result was that the median score was no higher regardless of whether the breadwinner was male or female. The explanation for this is, of course, that at the lower reaches of socioeconomic class the nature of the jobs—janitors, laundry workers, manual laborers—confer low prestige as well as low income. The female domestic and the male manual laborer are rated equally low in prestige in the inner city.

SCHOOL DATA

The nominated predelinquents were not only older, proportionately more often black, more frequently from one-parent homes, and of lower socioeconomic status but, as expected, their school functioning was also considerably poorer than the good-boy comparisons. This is reflected in IQ scores (in the sixth grade), test achievement scores, average grades received, and school attendence (see table 5).

IQ Scores

Although IQ scores do not necessarily measure what they are presumed to measure, particularly with deprived students, nevertheless they are certainly useful as a clue to performance. With regard to the 1,726 project subjects, the IQ scores obtained in the sixth grade were consistent for the three cohort years, but varied by nomination. Overall, the 632 experimental bad boys had an average IQ score of 91.6; the 462 bad-boy controls, 90.3; and the good-boy comparisons, 100.4. This 10-point superiority for the good-boy comparisons was consistent for each of the three cohort years. Thus, in 1963–64 the bad boys, both experimental and control, averaged 89.4 and 88.0, respectively, and the comparison subjects averaged 96.7. The following year the average IQ scores increased in each of the groups and were, in order, 92.8, 93.1, and 100.9. In the last year of intake the average scores were 92.4, 90.0, and 102.9, respectively (see table 5).

Reading Achievement

Achievement tests in reading and arithmetic, as well as IQ tests, were routinely administered to all sixth-grade students in the spring. The average reading achievement scores are shown in table 5. The 632 experimentals had an average reading grade level of 5.7, and it varied in the three cohort years from 5.3 to 6.0. The 462 controls had a mean grade level in reading of 5.5 and ranged by cohort year from 5.2 to 6.0. The 632 good-boy comparisons were over a year more advanced in reading grade level, namely 6.7 and varied from 6.5 to 7.1 in the three cohort years.

Arithmetic Achievement

As with reading and IQ test scores, but not quite so markedly, the nominated predelinquents were well below the nominated good boys in arithmetic grade-level achievement. The averages are shown in table 5. The experimental subjects had an average arithmetic achievement grade level of 6.3; the controls, 5.9; and the good-boy comparisons, 7.1. The variations within the three groups, by year of intake, appeared to be random. The range for the experimentals was from 5.7 to 6.8; the controls, from 5.4 to 6.5; and the comparisons, from 6.7 to 7.5. This intragroup variation, by year, was much greater on the arithmetic grade level than in the reading scores (see table 5).

Average Grade

Counting an A as 1 and an F as 5, the sixth-grade point average of each student in the study was computed. The experimentals and controls fell at 3.3 and 3.4 respectively (that is, C−), whereas the good-boy comparisons stood at exactly 2.5 (that is, B−). In short, the nominated bad boys averaged a letter grade poorer than the good boys. There was minimal variation by cohort year (see table 5).

School Attendance

The last indicator of school performance was in the regularity of attendance. To arrive at this index, a ratio between the number of school days present and the total number of school days was computed. This index was used instead of a simpler measure, such as the number of days absent, because it was a more stable figure and was recommended as such by Columbus school authorities. It avoids the problem of excused and unexcused absences.

On the basis of this ratio, both the 632 experimental subjects and the 462 controls attended classes 94% of the time, and the good boys were present 96% of the time. Here again, there were only minimal variations by year of intake into the demonstration program (see table 5).

POLICE CONTACTS

After obtaining the nominations and ratings by the sixth-grade teachers and the principals and the background data and school performance scores from the permanent record cards, the names of all 1,726 boys were routinely cleared for previous police contact with the Juvenile Bureau of the Columbus Police Department. The adequacy of such clearances, of course, is always subject to doubt, for the complaining and reporting processes are anything but uniform. Yet, other than self-reports, which are also subject to gross under- or over-reporting, police clearances are all that is available to researchers at this time. There is, however, a positive correlation between official reports and self-reports, particularly for the more serious offenses.

Of the total of 1,726 boys, 245 (14.2%) were known to the police by the time they entered the seventh grade. Both in the experimental and control groups, over 19% had experienced police contact. In contrast, only about 5% of the good-boy comparisons were known to the police prior to their entry into the project. These data are given in table 6.

The 125 experimental boys known to the police had experienced a total of 227 contacts, or approximately an average of 1.8 contacts. Of these 227 separate recorded events, 52 were relatively serious and 119 were moderately serious. Together, these offenses constitute the felonies and high misdemeanors. The remaining 56 contacts of the experimentals involved violations of city ordinances or of laws pertaining to minors in need of

TABLE 6

NUMBER AND PERCENTAGE OF EXPERIMENTALS, CONTROLS, AND
COMPARISONS HAVING HAD POLICE CONTACT PRIOR TO PROJECT

	EXPERI-MENTALS		CONTROLS		COM-PARISONS		TOTAL	
	N	%	N	%	N	%	N	%
Known to police......	125	19.8	88	19.1	32	5.1	245	14.2
Not known to police...	507	80.2	374	80.9	600	94.9	1,481	85.8
Total..............	632	100.0	462	100.0	632	100.0	1,726	100.0

supervision. The known contacts of the 88 control boys
prior to the seventh grade included 137 events (1.6 per
boy), of which 30 were of the serious kind, 78 were in
the moderate category, and 29 in the minor offense
group. In contrast, the 32 comparison boys with prior
contact were known for 39 offenses (1.2 per boy), 10
major, 18 moderate, and 11 minor (see table 7).

As noted in table 7, most of the serious offenses committed by all three groups of boys prior to the project
involved property rather than persons. Of the 92 recorded serious events, burglary and larceny predominated, although 18 of these 92 events had a person as
victim. Similarly, of the 215 events classified as moderate, over half were for petit larceny alone, and about
one-fifth were for vandalism involving destruction of
property valued at less than $50.00.

The minor violations as officially recorded on police
records included 14 different offenses: curfew violation, discharging a BB gun in the city, disorderly conduct, filing a false fire alarm or police report, fighting,
using improper language, incorrigibility, making men-
acing threats, throwing missiles, trespassing, home
and school truancy, general delinquency, and riding
double on a bicycle. Naturally, truancy, incorrigibility,
trespassing, and curfew violations predominated.

TABLE 7
TYPE OF POLICE CONTACT OF EXPERIMENTAL, CONTROL, AND COMPARISON
SUBJECTS, PRIOR TO ENTRANCE INTO THE PROJECT

OFFENSE TYPE	EXPERI-MENTAL	CONTROL	COM-PARISON	TOTAL
Serious				
Aggravated assault...............	...	1	..	1
Arson.........................	1	1	..	2
Assault and battery..............	2	1	1	4
Assault with a deadly weapon.....	4	...	..	4
Auto theft......................	2	4	..	6
Breaking and entering............	6	4	1	11
Burglary.......................	14	8	4	26
Grand larceny..................	3	1	..	4
Housebreaking..................	10	4	2	16
Molesting......................	3	...	..	3
Receiving and concealing stolen				
property......................	2	3	..	5
Theft from the mail..............	...	1	..	1
Unarmed robbery................	4	1	..	5
Vandalism; over $50 damage.......	1	1	1	3
Sodomy........................	...	...	1	1
Total.....................	52	30	10	92
Moderate				
Serious offense attempted or				
investigated...................	24	20	4	48
Carrying a concealed weapon......	1	...	..	1
Malicious destruction of property;				
under $50 damage.............	24	14	5	43
Petit larceny...................	66	41	7	114
Shoplifting.....................	2	1	..	3
Careless fire....................	...	1	..	1
Illicit sex with consent...........	...	...	1	1
Car tampering or stripping........	2	1	1	4
Total.....................	119	78	18	215
Slight				
Curfew violation.................	5	4	..	9
Discharging firearms in city				
limits (BB gun)...............	1	1	..	2
Disorderly conduct..............	3	...	2	5
False fire alarm, false report.......	3	2	1	6
Fighting.......................	2	2	..	4
Improper language..............	1	...	..	1
Incorrigibility..................	11	5	..	16
Menancing threats..............	1	...	..	1
Throwing missiles...............	1	...	1	2
Trespassing....................	2	5	4	11
Truancy from home.............	19	6	1	26
Truancy from school............	4	2	1	7
Delinquency...................	2	3	..	5
Riding double on bicycle..........	1	...	..	1
Total.....................	56	29	11	96
Grand total...............	227	137	39	403

This analysis of the study population yielded two principal results. First, the experimental and control subjects were, in fact, quite similar with regard to the demographic, school, and police data. As a group, the nominated bad boys, whether experimental or control, were different from the good-boy comparison subjects. The former—the nominated bad boys—were at least half a year older on the average, more often black, less frequently from intact families, and of lower socio-economic status. The school-data variables reveal that the bad boys, in relation to the good-boy comparisons, had nearly a 10-point IQ deficit on the average, were a year behind in reading grade level, were over half a year behind in arithmetic achievement, were a letter grade lower (C— versus B—) in average point-hour scores, and had poorer school-attendance records. With regard to police contacts prior to the seventh grade, the nominated bad boys were known proportionately about four times more often than the nominated good boys for both serious and minor offenses.

Second, although there was some variation in the demographic, school, and police data by year of intake into the program, this was mostly random in character. Thus, the 507 boys in the first year of the demonstration program were very much like the 544 in the second year and the 675 in the last year. As a result, the findings to be presented in the following chapters will be based on the total number of experimental, control, and comparison subjects without regard to year of intake.

PATTERNS IN BLACK AND WHITE

Not only were there significant differences in the demographic characteristics, school variables, and serious- and minor-police contacts between the nominated good and bad boys, but there were also patterns in black and white that emerged within these groups. First, as already noted, 51% of the experimentals and just over 50% of the controls were white. By contrast, of the randomly selected sample of good boys, 62% were white. For whatever reasons, and these can be readily enumerated, teachers and principals in the inner-city schools considered black students to be far more vulnerable to delinquent involvement.

The black and white nominees in each group were very different in many important respects. Some of these differences are presented in table 8. At the same time, color differences were frequently less significant than were the nominations as predelinquent or non-predelinquent.

Good boys, black and white alike, were about half a year younger than the experimental and control blacks and whites. On the other hand, family intactness was far greater for the white nominees in each group. Thus, 63.4%, 65.2%, and 72.4%, respectively, of the white experimental, control, and comparison subjects came from two-parent families in contrast to 46.1%, 46.7%, and 58.8% of the respective black students. By the same token, female-based households and surrogate family arrangements were more characteristic of the black boys in all three groups. For example, approximately 13% more black than white experimentals and controls and over 9% more black than white good boys were from female-based homes.

The intactness of the family was not related to its median socioeconomic status index score. In general, and as previously noted, both male and female lower-class unskilled and service jobs carry so little social

TABLE 8

CHARACTERISTICS OF WHITE AND BLACK EXPERIMENTAL, CONTROL, AND COMPARISON SUBJECTS, PRIOR TO ENTRANCE INTO THE PROJECT

	EXPERIMENTAL		CONTROL		COMPARISON	
	White	Black	White	Black	White	Black
Demographic						
Mean age	13.31	13.18	13.29	13.26	12.74	12.80
*Family composition**						
Intact	63.40	46.10	65.20	46.70	72.40	58.80
Female based	20.50	34.20	18.50	35.80	14.50	23.80
Surrogate	12.70	15.20	12.90	14.80	11.50	15.40
Other	3.40	4.50	3.40	2.70	1.60	2.00
Median socioeconomic status†						
All families	19	19	19	18	23	19
Male-headed families	19	18	19	17	25	19
School achievement						
Mean IQ	93.78	89.26	93.49	87.11	103.21	95.72
Mean reading achievement	5.90	5.47	5.89	5.18	7.10	6.12
Mean arithmetic achievement	6.37	6.14	6.19	5.51	7.40	6.54
Mean grade point‡	3.32	3.26	3.37	3.35	2.50	2.61
School attendance§	.93	.95	.93	.94	.96	.97

* Given in column percentages.
† According to the Reiss system based on the occupational prestige of the breadwinner's job.
‡ A = 1, B = 2, C = 3, D = 4, and F = 5.
§ Percent of days present out of the total number of school days.

prestige that whether the breadwinner is male or female is of little moment in this regard.

In school achievement, color was of some consequence. In all three groups—experimental, control, and good-boy comparison—white boys tested about five or more points higher on IQ. They were also uniformly higher in reading and arithmetic achievement-score averages. On the other hand, there were no real differences in average grade-point scores. The black boys in all three study groups also had better attendance records than their white counterparts.

Although these patterns by color have been consistently documented in the past, there is one aspect of our data that requires special notice. The black boys nominated as good by both their teachers and principals were consistently better on school measures than the white boys nominated as bad. They had higher IQ scores and were nearly a year ahead in both reading and arithmetic. Their grade point (B−) was one letter grade higher than that of the white predelinquents, and their class attendance record (97%) was greater than that of any other subgroup, black or white (see table 8).

Police clearances revealed no substantial racial differences in the percentages of experimental, control, and comparison boys previously known to the police, although the minor differences that did exist favored the white boys (see table 9).

The 64 white experimental subjects were recorded by the police for 106 separate delinquency events, of which over two-thirds were serious and moderate in character; the 61 black experimental subjects were known to the police for 121 separate events of which nearly 80% were serious and moderate. The 37 white

TABLE 9

NUMBER AND PERCENTAGE OF WHITE AND BLACK EXPERIMENTAL, CONTROL, AND COMPARISON SUBJECTS WITH POLICE CONTACT, PRIOR TO ENTRANCE INTO THE PROJECT, FOR ALL THREE COHORT YEARS

(1963–64, 1964–65, 1965–66)

| | EXPERIMENTALS | | | | CONTROLS | | | | COMPARISONS | | | |
| | White | | Black | | White | | Black | | White | | Black | |
	N	%	N	%	N	%	N	%	N	%	N	%
Known to the police	64	19.9	61	19.7	37	15.9	51	22.3	21	5.4	11	4.6
Not known to the police	258	80.1	249	80.3	196	84.1	178	77.7	371	94.6	229	95.4

controls were known for 196 delinquent acts and the 51 black controls for 178 such acts. In both cases, over two-thirds of the events were serious and moderate. Finally, the 21 white and 11 black comparison subjects had committed 25 and 14 offenses respectively, most of which were designated as serious and moderate (see table 10).

TABLE 10

DISTRIBUTION OF OFFENSES COMMITTED BY WHITE AND BLACK EXPERIMENTAL, CONTROL, AND COMPARISON SUBJECTS, PRIOR TO ENTRANCE INTO THE PROJECT, FOR ALL THREE COHORT YEARS (1963–64, 1964–65, 1965–66)

OFFENSE TYPE	EXPERIMENTALS		CONTROLS		COMPARISONS	
	White	Black	White	Black	White	Black
Serious	22	30	9	21	6	4
Moderate	51	68	25	53	11	7
Slight	33	23	14	15	8	3
Total	106	121	48	89	25	14

1. Walter C. Reckless, Simon Dinitz, and Ellen Murray, "Teacher Nominations and Evaluations of 'Good' Boys in High Delinquency Areas," *Elementary School Journal* 57 (1957):221.

2. Albert J. Reiss, Jr., *Occupations and Social Status* (New York: Free Press of Glencoe, 1961), Appendix B, p. 263.

CHAPTER SIX

Findings

The project design called for four yearly clearances of each boy through the files of the Juvenile Division of the Columbus Police Department and the files of the Columbus school system. The clearances were made once a year (in August) for four consecutive years. The three subgroups—experimentals, controls, and good-boy comparisons—of the 1963–64 cohort were cleared by name of each boy for any recorded delinquency, complaint, or arrest up to August 1964 and thereafter in each succeeding August through 1967. The three subgroups of the 1964–65 and 1965–66 cohorts were successively cleared following the same pattern.

Actually, cognizance was taken of any recorded complaints or arrests on each boy prior to entrance into the seventh grade (September) and for four consecutive years thereafter (each August). In the tables that follow, the time period called "during-program" means clearances during the period of the seventh grade (September until the middle of August), and the time period called "post-program" includes approximately three years of additional clearances.

For the purposes of this project, it had been decided that the most realistic criterion of official delinquency involvement would be a delinquency complaint or arrest registered in the files of the police, and that the use of police data for purposes of indicating outcome would be more satisfactory (less screened by subsequent decision-making) than the use of complaints referred by police and others to the juvenile court.

Other technical matters also need to be understood before presenting the clearance data. The tables that follow will be presented in terms of both the number of recorded events (complaints or arrests) and in terms of individual boys. It should be understood that the boys in the three subgroups (experimentals, controls, and comparisons) include all those on whom clearances could be made for each particular time period. The project was not able to follow up completely the cases of boys who were originally included in the three subgroups at the beginning of the seventh grade but who moved away from Columbus or who, for some other reason, became untraceable.

POLICE CONTACTS: EXPERIMENTALS, CONTROLS, AND COMPARISONS

Systematic monitoring of police records revealed that of the 632 experimental subjects, nearly 20% were known to the police prior to the program, 12% during the demonstration project, and nearly 38% became known during the three-year period following the program (see table 11). In all, nearly 48% had a record—at some time—either at the close of our follow-up or by the time they were about 16 years of age. For the controls, 462 in all, the percentages were nearly identical: 19% before, 11% during, 36% subsequent to the project, and 46% overall. Even the 632 good-boy comparisons fared rather poorly: 5%, 2%, 14%, and 18% respectively had contact with the police at some time during the years covered by the project.

TABLE 11

PERCENTAGES OF EXPERIMENT, CONTROL, AND COMPARISON BOYS
WITH POLICE CONTACT AT VARIOUS TIMES DURING THE STUDY

	EXPERI- MENTALS	CONTROLS	COMPARISONS
	*(632)	(462)	(632)
Pre-program......................	19.8	19.0	5.1
During program..................	12.3	10.8	1.9
Post-program....................	37.7	36.4	14.2
Overall.........................	47.8	46.3	18.4

* Denotes total number of subjects.

It must be noted that these contacts represent the minimal involvement of 1,726 boys in delinquent and criminal activities. This is so for three reasons. First, every study, particularly those on the self-reporting of deviant conduct, shows that the amount of involvement exceeds, by far, its official recording. The invisibility of much of the behavior and the unwillingness to report overt misconduct are well known. In addition, the modus operandi of the police and other agents in the juvenile justice system clearly serve to minimize the recording of juvenile offenders. Second, a considerable number of subjects had moved, and their delinquencies, if any, were recorded in other jurisdictions. Police-contact status covering all three time periods (pre-, during-, and post-program) could be assessed for 1,450, or 84%, of the original 1,726 boys. Of the 276 students who were lost through attrition (96 experimentals, 83 controls, and 97 good-boy comparisons), nearly 16%

had been known to the police prior to their loss from the study. Third, and a sad commentary on our system, is the pettiness of the offenses committed by many of the 1,726 subjects that led to their listing in the police files. To be stigmatized with a police record in adolescence may or may not have any serious consequences for lower-class youth; but to be stigmatized with such a record for the most minor of violations is, however, quite a different matter and grossly complicates the functioning of the juvenile justice system.

The original 1,726 subjects, including the 1,450 (536 experimentals, 379 controls, and 535 comparisons) for whom police-contact status could be assessed, were known to the police for 1,822 specific events. As table 12 reveals, nearly 30% of all recorded events were serious; 33.7% were classified as moderate; and 36.9%, as slight. Most of these criminal and delinquent acts, naturally enough, were committed in the post-project phase during the years of greatest vulnerability of adolescents to delinquency, namely 14–16 years of age. See Appendix C. Whether experimental, control, or comparison boys, most of the delinquent events recorded by the police occurred after the seventh grade (post-program) (see table 13).

The table presented in Appendix C lists all of the recorded offenses for which the original 1,726 boys were known. The single most often recorded offense was petit larceny, with 270 such entries. The next most frequent offense involved 199 violations in which a serious offense was either attempted or investigated. The third most numerous offense was auto theft (177 notations), followed by incorrigibility (167), curfew violation (157), and truancy from home (111). No other delinquencies exceeded 100 entries in number.

Using the Part 1 offense category of the Crime Index of the Uniform Crime Reports, there were: 2 murders (one by an experimental and the other by a good-boy comparison); no forcible rapes; 3 armed and 23 unarmed robberies; 13 aggravated assaults (and 50 assault and battery entries); 146 burglaries and/or breaking and entering events (and 35 house-breakings); 26 grand larcenies; and, as noted above, 177 auto thefts (see Appendix C).

In contrast, the 672 slight offenses involved not only incorrigibility, home truancy, and curfew violations but also disorderly conduct (28), intoxication (25), trespassing (40), and one violation each of shooting pool, riding double on a bike, unlawful assembly, and misrepresentation of minor status (see table 12 and Appendix C).

TABLE 12

NUMBER AND PERCENTAGE OF DELINQUENCY OFFENSES RECORDED
BY THE POLICE, CLASSIFIED AS SERIOUS, MODERATE, AND SLIGHT*

	EXPERIMENTALS		CONTROLS		COMPARISONS		TOTAL	
	N	%	N	%	N	%	N	%
Serious......	275	28.8	199	30.6	62	28.7	536	29.4
Moderate....	337	35.3	209	32.1	68	31.5	614	33.7
Slight.......	343	35.9	243	37.3	86	39.8	672	36.9
Total......	955	100.0	651	100.0	216	100.0	1,822	100.0

* Based on the tabulations for the specific offenses presented in Appendix C.

The data on the serious, moderate, and slight events mirror fairly accurately the juvenile crime problem in the United States. They present no surprises, unless the overexpected involvement in criminal activities by the nominated good-boys would be considered a surprise. See tables 12, 13, and Appendix C for the recorded involvement of the good-boy comparisons.

TABLE 13

Percentage of Delinquency Offenses Recorded by the Police, Classified as Serious, Moderate, and Slight, by Project Period*

	Experimentals			Controls			Comparisons			Total		
	Pre	During	Post	Pre	During	Post	Pre	During	Post	Pre	During	Post
Serious...........	18.9	14.2	66.9	15.1	15.1	69.8	16.1	6.5	77.4	17.2	13.6	69.2
Moderate...........	35.3	23.4	41.3	37.8	20.1	42.1	26.5	14.7	58.8	35.2	21.3	43.5
Slight...........	16.3	11.4	72.3	11.9	11.1	77.0	12.8	2.3	84.9	14.3	10.1	75.6
Total...........	23.8	16.4	59.8	21.2	15.2	63.6	18.1	7.4	74.5	22.2	14.9	62.9

* Based on the data in Appendix C.

POLICE CONTACTS: WHITE AND BLACK

Much has been written concerning the differential involvement of white and black boys in delinquency. The generally higher official rates of black adolescents have been explained in a variety of ways, depending largely on the perspective and orientation of the interpreters. More grinding poverty, more limited legitimate opportunities, greater status frustration, differential patterns of criminal justice, lesser family cohesion, a paucity of male role-models, and any number of other sociocultural, psychological, and even biological explanations have been suggested.

Approximately half of the experimental and control students were black, but only 38% of the nominated good-boy comparisons were black. Prior to the school-intervention program, the black control boys had a slightly more frequent involvement with the law than the white controls, an almost identical frequency in the experimental group, and a somewhat lesser frequency among the good-boy comparisons. The results show approximately the same pattern of white and black student delinquency during and after the program as prior to it in each of the three cohorts (see table 14).

Although there was no greater representation of black students by frequency of contact, the number of the offenses recorded for them was greater and the nature of the acts seemed more serious (see table 15). The black experimental students, constituting about half of the group, were known for 64.4% of the serious offenses. In the control group, in which the black boys comprised about half of the subjects, they accounted

TABLE 14

PERCENTAGES OF WHITE AND BLACK EXPERIMENTAL, CONTROL,
AND COMPARISON BOYS WITH POLICE CONTACT AT
VARIOUS TIMES DURING THE STUDY

	EXPERIMENTALS		CONTROLS		COMPARISONS	
	White	Black	White	Black	White	Black
Pre-program	19.9	19.7	15.9	22.3	5.4	4.6
During program	8.4	16.5	6.0	15.7	1.3	2.9
Post-program	32.3	43.2	28.8	44.1	13.0	16.3
Overall	44.1	51.6	39.0	53.7	16.8	20.8

for 73.9% of the serious offenses. In the comparison group, in which black representation was 38%, exactly half of the serious offenses were recorded for the black boys. Much the same pattern prevailed for the moderate offenses: black experimentals accounted for two-thirds of them; black controls, for 70%; and the black good boys for roughly 45%. On the other hand, the pattern with regard to the minor offenses is inconsistent. Black experimentals committed fewer slight offenses than expected, black controls were again over-represented; and the black good-boy comparisons were, like the experimentals, underrepresented.

On the Crime Index basis, the two reported murders were committed by a white experimental and a white good-boy comparison. Although there were no forcible rapes, 23 of the 28 armed and unarmed robberies were recorded for the black students. The aggravated, felonious, and deadly weapon assaults were evenly divided between blacks and whites; but the assault and battery events, which are not part of the FBI Crime Index, were heavily concentrated among the blacks. Burglaries, breaking and entering, and housebreaking offenses were very heavily registered against the blacks,

TABLE 15

Number and Percentage of Delinquency Offenses Recorded by the Police, Classified as Serious, Moderate, and Slight, by Race

| | Experimentals | | | | Controls | | | | Comparisons | | | |
| | White | | Black | | White | | Black | | White | | Black | |
	N	%	N	%	N	%	N	%	N	%	N	%
Serious.	97	24.3	178	32.0	52	24.3	147	33.6	31	24.0	31	35.6
Moderate.	112	28.1	225	40.5	63	29.4	146	33.4	38	29.5	30	34.5
Slight.	190	47.6	153	27.5	99	46.3	144	33.0	60	46.5	26	29.9
Total.	399	100.0	556	100.0	214	100.0	437	100.0	129	100.0	87	100.0

but the grand larcenies were undifferentiated by color. Auto thefts, surprisingly, were very much more concentrated among the blacks (see Appendix D).

In the moderate-offense group, black students were recorded about two-and-a-half times more often for the so-called Any serious offense attempted or investigated than their proportion in the study would demand by chance alone. The blacks were also disproportionately overrepresented for petit larceny and even more disproportionately for carrying a concealed weapon. The total numbers in the remainder of the moderate-offense category were too small to evaluate except to say that the black-white differences were small (see Appendix D).

In the minor-offense category, black-white differences were generally proportionate to the relative number of black and white subjects in the total study. Except for truancy from home, in which the white boys were greatly overrepresented in the experimental cohort, color was without significance for all other recorded delinquent activities. Incorrigibility, school truancies, and intoxication offenses are cases in point (see Appendix D).

POLICE-CONTACT CATEGORIES: TEACHER NOMINATIONS

In examining the delinquency involvement of the experimental, control, and comparison boys, regardless of race, several interesting subgroups emerged. These subcategories, which hereafter will be called police-contact categories, demonstrated again that predictions of law-violational behavior and of non-law-violational conduct, even by teachers who know their students well, can be hazardous. On the basis of known police contacts only, teacher nominations of boys *likely* or *possible* to get into later trouble with the law were gross overestimates (Type I error). Less frequent but still constituting a very substantial proportion of the nominees were boys nominated by their sixth-grade teachers as *unlikely* who did, in fact, experience police contact (Type II error).

These errors raise anew the unresolved issue of why it is that, despite every manner of social and economic adversity, the largest percentage of adolescent boys remain free from official legal involvement. The data that follow also pinpoint the dilemma of labeling adolescents as pre- or nondelinquent and of intervening on behalf of the former. Certainly, the arguments about the consequences of stigmatization raised by the "labeling school" of sociologists, including Goffman, Becker, Garfinkel, Szasz, Scheff, Kitsuse, Cicourel, and others, are pertinent to these data.

Simply stated, and as shown in table 16, 10 subcategories of experimental, control, and comparison subjects emerged: Category 1 consisted of boys wholly free from recorded delinquencies; Category 2, free from contact before and during the project but became known to the police in the post-project years; Category 3, free from contact before and after the project; Category 4, contact during and after the program but not before; Category 5, contact only before the program; Category 6, contact both before and after but not during the demonstration year; Category 7, contact before and during the program but not afterward; Category 8, contact in all three time periods—before, during, and after (really a hard-core group) ; Category 9, no contact before the program and only incomplete data available on them during and/or after the program;

and Category 10, contact before the program and incomplete data on them during and/or after the project.

TABLE 16

DISTRIBUTION OF EXPERIMENTAL, CONTROL, AND COMPARISON
SUBJECTS ACCORDING TO CATEGORY OF POLICE CONTACT

CATEGORY*	EXPERIMENTALS		CONTROLS		COMPARISONS	
	N	%	N	%	N	%
1	256	40.5	180	39.0	426	67.4
2	140	22.2	99	21.4	75	11.9
3	13	2.1	10	2.2	5	0.8
4	24	3.8	17	3.7	4	0.6
5	27	4.3	18	3.9	13	2.1
6	35	5.5	32	6.9	9	1.4
7	2	0.3	3	0.6	1	0.2
8	39	6.2	20	4.3	2	0.3
9	74	11.7	68	14.7	90	14.2
10	22	3.5	15	3.2	7	1.1
Total	632	100.0	462	100.0	632	100.0

* See above, p. 98.

SOCIAL CHARACTERISTICS OF THE POLICE-CONTACT
CATEGORIES

The age, color, class, and family-status distributions of the 632 experimental, 462 control, and 632 good-boy comparison subjects have been described in the preceding chapter. The purpose of this analysis is to indicate that the demographic characteristics of the offense categories varied significantly, with the exception of social class—since all subjects resided in the inner city.

Age

At the time of intake into the Youth Development Project, the mean age of the experimentals and controls was approximately 13.25 years, and that of the comparisons was 12.76. With regard to the police-contact category, however, the no-contact boys were 12.97 years at the start of the study and the hard-core delinquents (with police contact before, during, and after the project) averaged 13.69 years of age (see table 17). Within the no-contact category, the experimentals, controls, and comparison boys were 13.20, 13.23, and 12.73 years of age on the average. In the hard-core group, the experimentals, controls, and good-boy comparisons were 13.56, 13.95, and 13.50 years of age respectively.

In short, the more serious the police contact generally, the higher the mean age of the boys at the time of entry into the Youth Development Project. Further, within each contact category, the nominated predelinquents were older than the nominated good boys. The only exceptions occurred in those categories in which the number of cases was very small.

Whether the higher age of the more serious delinquents (police-contact cases) was the cause or the effect is, of course, subject to conjecture. There is no question, however, that the more serious police-contact cases were having a more difficult time in school—even in grade school.

Race

The patterns of police contact (delinquency involvement) according to race of the boy have been discussed previously. It should suffice, at this point, to suggest that there was a slightly greater proportion of whites in the no-contact group and a much greater proportion of black students in the hard-core delinquent category. The respective percentages, namely 54.6 and 31.7, indicate the gradient of color by offense category (see table

17, column 2). Although far from perfect as a gradient, the evidence is reasonably compelling that a greater proportion of the black subjects fell into the more-persistent-offender categories.

Family Status

The evidence on family status indicates that the no-contact subjects, whether experimental, control, or comparison, were derived more often from intact family constellations than were boys in all other groups. To illustrate the point, it is only necessary to compare again the two extreme groups—the no-contact (Category 1) group with the persistent-police-contact group (Category 8). In the former, 65.1% of all the students came from intact family settings and only 21.3% from female-based households. In the latter group, only half came from intact homes, and 35.0% lived in female-based households. Here again, however, it should be noted that in nearly every contact category a higher percentage of nominated good boys lived in intact households (see table 17, columns 3, 4, and 5).

SPECIFIC RECORDED OFFENSES

Of the 1,726 subjects in the project, 862 students (40.5% of the experimentals, 39.0% of the controls, and 67.4% of the good-boy comparisons) were wholly free from police contact (see table 18). These constitute the Category 1 boys, about whom more will be said later. For the present, it need only be pointed out that the teachers and principals were wrong about 2 in 5 of those whom they nominated as headed for trouble with the law or about whom they were uncertain.

TABLE 17

AGE, RACE, AND FAMILY STATUS BY POLICE-CONTACT CATEGORY

CATEGORY*	MEAN AGE	PERCENTAGE WHITE	FAMILY STATUS		
			Intact	Female-based	Other
1..............	12.97	54.6	65.1	21.3	13.6
2..............	13.02	48.7	57.0	26.7	16.3
3..............	13.48	25.0	46.4	21.4	32.2
4..............	13.41	37.8	48.9	24.4	26.7
5..............	13.27	60.3	53.4	25.9	20.7
6..............	13.47	43.4	46.1	38.1	15.8
7..............	12.77	50.0	50.0	16.7	33.3
8..............	13.69	31.7	50.0	35.0	15.0
9..............	13.02	76.3	56.9	19.9	23.2
10..............	13.50	72.7	54.5	31.8	13.7

* See above, p. 98.

By the same token, the nominators were in error about 1 in 3 of their good-boy nominees. The 314 boys in Category 2 included roughly 22% of the 1,094 nominated predelinquents and 12% of the 632 nominated good boys. These students were free from contact prior to and during the program but came to the attention of the police thereafter. As may be seen in table 18, they were known for 619 offenses, an average of 1.97 police notations per boy in this group. Their 10 most frequent offenses, constituting 34% of all recorded events, were curfew violation (81), auto theft (80), incorrigibility (59), petit larceny (52), truancy from home (46), attempted serious offenses (38), burglary (27), malicious destruction of property (21), breaking and entering (20), assault and battery (19), and trespassing (19). Category 3 boys (those with police contacts during the program only) numbered 28 and accounted for 2.1% of the nominated predelinquents and less than 1% of the nominated good boys. As table 18 indicates, these 28 boys were known for 36 offenses collectively or 1.29 each. All of their offenses were recorded during the seventh grade only and consisted of the following: attempted serious offenses and petit larceny (6 each), and incorrigibility and the malicious destruction of property (5 each). No other offense was reported more than twice.

Category 4 boys (having contacts during and after the program) were 45 in number and included about 3.7% of the predelinquent nominees but only 0.6% of the nominated good boys. They were responsible for over four violations each (4.27) and appeared headed for continued trouble. Their records revealed the following distribution of recorded offenses: petit larceny (31), auto theft (20), incorrigibility (19), attempted serious offense (18), and curfew violation (16). The only other violation accounting for more than 10 events was assault and battery (14).

Category 5 subjects (police contacts prior to this study but not thereafter) numbered 58 and included 4% of the nominated predelinquents and 2.1% of the nominated good boys. These 58 boys were responsible for 77 violations (4.2% of the total recorded offenses), an average of 1.33 notations per boy. Petit larceny (19) and attempted serious offense (10) were the only notations exceeding 10 in number and were followed in order of frequency by burglary, malicious destruction of property, and home truancy.

Category 6 boys (police contacts before and after, but not during, the program) numbered 76. Their 288 violations (15.8% of the grand total) constituted an average of 3.79 per boy. About 6% of the nominated predelinquents (experimentals and controls) and over 1% of the good-boy comparisons were included in this group. Again, petit larceny (44), attempted offense

(34), curfew violations (30), and auto theft (21) led the list of recorded events.

Category 7 consisted of boys who were known to the police only before and during the project. These 6 cases accounted for 15 offenses. Category 8 contained the hard-core delinquents (boys with police contact before, during, and after the project). These 61 boys, about 5% of the nominated predelinquents and only 0.3% of the good-boy nominees, committed 499 violations. These recorded events represented 27.4% of all known offenses, an average of 8.18 recorded offenses per boy, as may be noted in table 18. These 61 subjects committed at least one of 43 separate offenses, from murder to glue-sniffing. Despite this wide range, the major notations were very much the same as for the others who had experienced police contact. Petit larceny (93), attempted serious offense (79), incorrigibility (56), auto theft (50), and burglary (34) were the five leading violations in Category 8.

Categories 9 and 10, consisted of 276 boys. Data on their involvement during and/or after the study are, by definition, incomplete. Such findings as are known are presented in table 18.

SCHOOL DATA

Viewed objectively, the experimental subjects, as a result of exposure to the Youth Development program, did not display any more favorable school performance than the boys not exposed (the controls and comparisons). In general, the experimentals and controls neither gained nor lost ground to the good boys. The data suggest that the nominated good boys fell considerably in their performance, just about as much as the nomi-

TABLE 18

NUMBER OF BOYS, NUMBER AND PERCENTAGE OF RECORDED OFFENSES,
AND MEAN NUMBER OF OFFENSES, BY POLICE-CONTACT CATEGORY

CATEGORY	NUMBER OF BOYS	OFFENSES		MEAN NUMBER OF OFFENSES
		N	%	
1.	862	...	...	...
2.	314	619	34.0	1.97
3.	28	36	2.0	1.29
4.	45	192	10.5	4.27
5.	58	77	4.2	1.33
6.	76	288	15.8	3.79
7.	6	15	0.8	2.50
8.	61	499	27.4	8.18
9.	232	20	1.1	0.09
10.	44	76	4.2	1.73
Total.	1,726	1,822	100.0	...

* See above, p. 98.

nated predelinquents, so that the differential between
the two groups of nominees (predelinquent and nondelinquent) remained consistent from the sixth through
the tenth grades.

FINAL SCHOOL-CLEARANCE STATUS

At the conclusion of the follow-up, school clearances
indicated that 56.6% of the experimentals, 51.3% of
the controls, and 77.1% of the good-boy comparisons
were still in school. In contrast, 19.1%, 22.7%, and
6.2% respectively of the experimental, control, and
good-boy subjects were school dropouts by the end of
the tenth grade (see table 19). In this respect, then,
the program may have had a favorable impact in preventing a few additional dropouts among the experimentals. The difference is so small, however, that
chance alone, to say nothing of those who had moved
away and on whom our data were therefore incomplete,

TABLE 19

SCHOOL STATUS OF EXPERIMENTAL, CONTROL, AND COMPARISON
SUBJECTS AT THE END OF THE PROJECT

SCHOOL STATUS	EXPERIMENTALS	CONTROLS	COMPARISONS
	*(632)	(462)	(632)
In school.................	56.6	51.3	77.1
Dropout..................	19.1	22.7	6.2
Moved away..............	18.6	20.8	16.1
In custody...............	5.7	5.2	0.6
Total.................	100.0	100.0	100.0

* Denotes total number of subjects.

could have produced this minor positive result. The school outcome data are presented above.

A more incisive way of looking at the relationship between the two principal goals of the project, namely, the prevention of delinquency and the prevention of school dropout, is to look at the two simultaneously by using offense category or type. When this is done, the contrast, presented in table 20, between the police-contact and no-police-contact groups is very pronounced. Those boys who experienced difficulty with the law were school dropouts in far greater proportion than those without contact. Both school dropout and police contacts seem to derive from the same configuration and hence are highly interrelated. The school dropout gradient for all groups is clearly visible in table 20.

Concentrating attention on only three of the 10 police-contact categories demonstrates the relationship between the two dependent variables. Of the boys who never had any police contact (Category 1), 82.8%, 79.4%, and 95.8% of the 256 experimentals, 180 controls, and 426 good-boy comparisons were still in school at the end of the follow-up (three years after the

TABLE 20

Percentage Distribution of Final School-clearance Status by Police-contact Category

CATEGORY*	Experimentals			Controls			Comparisons		
	In School	Dropout	Other†	In School	Dropout	Other†	In School	Dropout	Other†
1	82.8	17.2	...	79.4	20.6	...	95.8	4.2	...
2	62.1	22.1	15.7	49.5	36.4	14.2	73.3	18.7	8.0
3	76.9	23.1	...	50.0	50.0	...	100.0	...	...
4	29.2	29.2	41.6	47.1	35.3	17.7	75.0	25.0	...
5	51.9	48.1	...	61.1	38.9	...	84.6	15.4	...
6	51.4	34.3	14.3	53.1	25.0	21.8	33.3	33.3	33.3
7	100.0	...	...	66.7	33.3	...	100.0	...	...
8	21.1	28.9	50.0	10.0	25.0	65.0	50.0	50.0	...
9	...	...	100.0	...	...	100.0	...	...	100.0
10	...	...	100.0	...	...	100.0	...	...	100.0

* See above, p. 98.
† Other includes those who moved away or are in custody.

seventh grade). Of the 27 experimental, 18 control, and 13 good boys who had contact before but not during or after the program (Category 5), 51.9%, 61.1%, and 84.6% respectively were still in school. In stark contrast, only 21.1% of the experimentals and 10.0% of the controls in Category 8 were still in school, as was 1 of the 2 nominated good boys. Thus, 88.5% of the no-contact boys, 62.1% of those with police contact before the study only, and 18.3% of those in trouble during all of the three time periods were attending school at the close of the follow-up.

SCHOOL ATTENDANCE

Inevitably, school attendance reflects motivation, goals, and perceptions of the legitimacy and the significance of the educational institution. (See chapter 7 for an analysis of the attitudes of the students toward various aspects of school.) In examining the hard data on school truancy and attendance, several findings were evident. First, the experimental and control subjects did not differ from each other before, during, or after the project (see table 21). Second, at all grade levels, the good-boy comparisons were less truant than the nominated predelinquents, whether experimental or control. Third, and last, in all three groups attendance declined with age. As the experimental, control, and comparison boys moved through the seventh, eighth, ninth, and tenth grades, truancy increased markedly. This increase occurred in spite of the increase in dropout by grade, which removed the hard-core school truants.

Not at all surprising was the finding that school attendance varied with offense category. In fact, all

TABLE 21

ATTENDANCE RATIOS OF EXPERIMENTAL, CONTROL, AND COMPARISON
BOYS FROM THE SIXTH THROUGH THE TENTH GRADE

ATTENDANCE RATIO	EXPERIMENTALS	CONTROLS	COMPARISONS
Sixth grade..................	.937	.936	.961
Seventh grade...............	.929	.927	.955
Eighth grade................	.908	.913	.951
Ninth grade.................	.906	.906	.944
Tenth grade.................	.866	.869	.919

three results discussed immediately above applied to
the offenses-category analysis as well. In each offense
category, that is, 1 to 10, the experimentals and controls had a similar pattern; the nominated good boys
were better school attenders, and attendance ratios declined with grade level. In the tenth grade, for example, the attendance ratio of the no-contact boys
(Category 1) was .915; for the before group only
(Category 5) it was .867; and for the hard-core group
(Category 8), the ratio was only .669. Rather than
present the table in its entirety, the mean attendance
ratios by grade and offense category are presented for
all cohorts combined in table 22 below.

TABLE 22

MEAN ATTENDANCE RATIOS BY SCHOOL GRADE AND
POLICE-CONTACT CATEGORY

CATEGORY*	SIXTH GRADE	SEVENTH GRADE	EIGHTH GRADE	NINTH GRADE	TENTH GRADE
1................	.958	.953	.945	.939	.915
2................	.942	.930	.907	.896	.836
3................	.922	.914	.937	.928	.871
4................	.917	.910	.879	.868	.738
5................	.939	.930	.917	.892	.867
6................	.899	.920	.894	.866	.833
7................	.960	.929	.970	.953	.879
8................	.916	.867	.800	.863	.669
9................	.941	.932	.919	.907	...
10................	.912	.902	.853	.916	...

* See above, p. 98.

SCHOOL GRADES

An evaluation of school grade points (A, B, C, D, E) reinforces the previous analyses of school dropout and truancy. As before, the mean grade-point scores did not differ for the experimentals and controls; the good-boy nominees did better than the nominated bad boys throughout; and average grade-point scores fell with time. These results are presented in table 23.

TABLE 23

MEAN GRADE-POINT AVERAGES OF EXPERIMENTAL, CONTROL, AND COMPARISON SUBJECTS, BEFORE, DURING, AND AFTER THE PROGRAM

GRADE AVERAGE*	EXPERIMENTALS	CONTROLS	COMPARISONS
Pre-program (6th grade)..	3.29	3.36	2.54
During program (7th grade)...............	3.33	3.48	2.93
Post-program (8th, 9th, and 10th grades).......	3.64	3.55	3.11

* A = 1, B = 2, C = 3, D = 4, and F = 5.

Mean grade-point averages varied consistently, and in the predicted direction, with the offense category. The no-contact subjects, whether experimental, control, or comparison, did better in school than the hard-core (Category 8) delinquents; all other categories were intermediate between these extremes. For the no-contact cases, the means were 2.89, 3.05, and 3.23 in the three periods under study (the pre-, during-, and post-project phases). However, within the no-police-contact category, the experimentals, controls, and comparisons averaged 3.20, 3.35, and 2.49 in the pre-program; 3.19, 3.31, and 2.86 during the project; and 3.53, 3.38, and 3.03 in the follow-up period. The grade-point averages by police-contact category are presented in table 24.

TABLE 24

MEAN GRADE-POINT AVERAGES BY POLICE-CONTACT CATEGORY

CATEGORY*	PRE-PROGRAM	DURING-PROGRAM	POST-PROGRAM
1	2.89	3.05	3.23
2	3.15	3.41	3.76
3	3.16	3.50	3.35
4	3.56	3.74	4.07
5	3.09	3.36	3.52
6	3.42	3.54	3.82
7	3.31	3.42	3.78
8	3.38	3.56	3.88
9	3.02	3.22	...
10	3.48	3.42	...

* See above, p. 98.

SUMMARY

In summary, the police and school data unfortunately failed to sustain the hope that the Youth Development Project would effectively prevent delinquency involvement and school dropout among inner-city boys. Instead, every measure indicated little or no difference between the treated and untreated nominated predelinquents. Also dismaying was the increasing frequency with age of recorded delinquencies among the nominated good boys, the concomitant decline in their school grades and school attendance, and the accompanying increase in their school dropout rate.

These results, although negating the intervention efforts of the project, were most revealing in other respects. When the subjects were classified by categories of police contact, from no-contact to hard core, the differences on the demographic and school-clearance variables were highly significant in the expected direction.

CHAPTER SEVEN

Attitude and Perception Changes

In addition to accumulating systematic police-clearance data and school-record information on the progress of each of our 1,726 experimental, control, and comparison subjects, the project attempted to evaluate attitudinal and perceptional changes in the boys during the year of the intervention program.

THE FIRST COHORT, 1963–64[1]

In order to test the effects of the first year of intervention, a schedule or questionnaire was devised that included measures of socialization, self-concept, and interpersonal competence (see schedule in Appendix E). The schedule contained five sections. The first, entitled "How I Feel About Things," consisted of 15 of the original 54 items in the Harrison Gough Socialization Scale, which is a subscale of the California Psychological Inventory. These 15 items had been found to be the most sensitive for measuring the veering toward or away from delinquency, based on the previous work of the investigators in the schools. High scorers on the Socialization Scale (SO) scale are more likely to be serious, honest, and responsible, whereas low scorers have been found to be more negative, undependable, and delinquency-prone. There is a large literature on the complete SO scale, indicating the differential response profiles of criteria groups, ranging from best citizens to institutionalized and seriously delinquent boys.

For the sake of simplicity and the facilitation of administration, a short form of the investigators' self-concept inventory was included as the second section of the schedule. This section contained 7 items of the original 56, selected precisely because they had been found to be the most discriminating in regard to teacher nominations as well as in differentiating the high and low scorers on the SO scale.

The third set of items in the schedule administered to the first cohort was drawn from Edward Rothstein's attempt to measure interpersonal competence and the ability of adolescents to interact effectively with others in social situations. Composed originally of 60 items in 6 subscales, Rothstein's Q-sort analysis revealed that 11 of these questions differentiated delinquents and nondelinquents. These 11 items purport to measure interpersonal competence in the areas of judgment, intelligence, health, empathy, and creativity.

The schedule also contained the 20 Statements Test, or "Who Am I?", developed by Manford Kuhn. The "Who Am I?" test is based on certain assumptions central to symbolic interaction theory. As with other projective tests, it was difficult to analyze reliably the "20 Statements," and this test was abandoned after the first year (see Appendix E).

This complete schedule—the SO, the self-concept, the interpersonal competence, and the "Who Am I?" items—was administered to all sixth-grade boys in the 44 feeder schools by their own teachers in the spring of the school year preceding the intervention program. To measure the attitudinal and perceptual impact of the program, the same schedule was readministered the following spring after the school-demonstration work was completed. Although all sixth-grade boys in the 44 feeder schools were tested, only the experimentals and controls were retested. The good boys were not retested because to do so would have revealed to the school administration their status as comparison subjects. In addition, since only a 15% sample of the good-boy comparisons was taken to begin with, reaching them for retesting would have impaired the research.

The results of this pre- and post-testing were disheartening and resulted in specific modifications in our curriculum emphasis in the second and third years. Specifically, the presentations in the lesson plans dealing with the worlds of School, Work, and the Family were strengthened; more attention was given to the reading program; and greater stress was placed on the teachers as role models.

THE SO SCALE TEST-RETEST RESULTS

On the 15 items of the Socialization Scale (SO), the boys who later were randomly selected as experimentals and controls scored on an average (mean) 8.51 and 8.63, respectively, whereas the good boys had a significantly more favorable score of 10.0. (High scores on the socialization items are in the favorable, low scores in the unfavorable, direction.) Both the experimentals and controls showed higher (better) post-test mean scores (see table 25). The experimental boys

TABLE 25

MEAN SCORES ON 15 ITEMS OF THE SOCIALIZATION SCALE, PRE- AND POST-TEST, BY SUBGROUPS IN THE 1963–64 COHORT

	PRE-TEST	POST-TEST	P*
Experimentals....................	8.51	8.97	NS
Controls........................	8.63	9.26	NS
Comparisons....................	10.00	†	

* P denotes level of statistical significance.
† Not administered.

(195) who took the pre- and post-tests moved up to a mean of 8.97; the control boys (100), to 9.26. Neither increase, although in the expected direction, was statistically significant. However, the controls unexpectedly did better than the experimentals on the retest. These differences could be explained by chance alone, and the improvement by test-retest learning and greater sophistication.

An item analysis revealed that there was no single item among the 15 socialization items on which both experimentals and controls improved significantly in the post-test. However, on items 4 and 7 the experimentals showed significant improvement (see table 26). These two items are:

4. I seem to do things that I regret more often than other people do.

7. I go out of my way to try to meet trouble rather than escape it.

The controls had significantly higher mean post-test scores on the following items (see table 26) :

2. I used to give the teachers lots of trouble.

TABLE 26

EXTENT OF CHANGE IN THE PERCENTAGE OF SUBJECTS SCORING
FAVORABLY ON THE 15 SOCIALIZATION ITEMS,
PRE- AND POST-TEST, 1963–64

ITEM NUMBER	EXPERIMENTALS			CONTROLS		
	Pre-test	Post-test	% Change	Pre-test	Post-test	% Change
	*(206)	(195)		(108)	(100)	
1..........	82.0	88.7	+ 6.7	82.4	83.8	+ 1.4
2‡.........	35.9	36.9	+ 1.0	36.4	49.0	+12.6
3..........	79.2	78.2	− 1.0	83.2	73.7	− 9.5
4†.........	45.1	56.4	+11.3	51.9	47.5	− 4.4
5..........	65.9	74.9	− 9.0	63.0	69.7	+ 6.7
6..........	48.1	47.2	− .9	44.4	45.5	+ 1.1
7†.........	59.6	78.9	+19.3	71.0	76.5	+ 5.5
8‡.........	20.4	20.5	+ .1	32.4	15.3	−17.1
9..........	34.5	26.7	− 7.8	30.6	38.4	+ 7.8
10‡........	33.5	37.1	+ 3.6	34.6	50.0	+15.4
11.........	83.5	83.9	+ .4	86.1	87.9	+ 1.8
12.........	90.2	88.7	− 1.5	88.0	92.9	+ 4.9
13‡........	35.1	43.8	+ 8.7	31.8	51.5	+19.7
14.........	64.9	72.2	+ 7.3	63.0	71.7	+ 8.7
15‡........	59.7	61.9	+ 2.2	56.5	70.7	+14.2

* Denotes number of subjects.
† Change in experimental group at .05 or better.
‡ Change in control group at .05 or better.

8. When I meet a stranger, I often think he is better than I am.

10. I keep out of trouble at all costs.

13. People often talk about me behind my back.

15. I never cared much for school.

Further analysis also showed that the experimentals did more poorly on items 7 and 8 on the pre-test than did the controls. In the post-test situation, however, the experimentals did significantly more poorly on items 2 and 10 and on item 9 ("I was sometimes sent to the principal for cutting up") (see table 26).

SELF-CONCEPT-SCALE RESULTS

It was expected that the impact of the project would be reflected in the pre- and post-test scores of the experimental and control subjects on the self-concept inventory, consisting of 7 items. There appeared, however, to be no significant improvement in the mean scores of either group at the end of the school year.

TABLE 27

MEAN SCORES ON THE 7 SELF-CONCEPT ITEMS,
PRE- AND POST-TEST, EXPERIMENTAL AND
CONTROL SUBJECTS, 1963–64

	PRE-TEST	POST-TEST	P*
Experimentals.............	9.38	9.61	NS
Controls.................	9.54	9.45	NS
P*.......................	NS	NS	

* P denotes level of statistical significance.

There was also no significant difference in mean scores between the two groups either before or after the program. The mean scores on these 7 self-concept items are shown in table 27.

Analysis of each of the 7 self-concept items revealed no significant changes within the experimental and control groups over the one-year period. Analysis also

TABLE 28

EXTENT OF CHANGE IN THE PERCENTAGE OF SUBJECTS
SCORING FAVORABLY ON 7 SELF-CONCEPT ITEMS,
PRE- AND POST-TEST, 1963–64

ITEM NUMBER	EXPERIMENTALS			CONTROLS		
	Pre-test	Post-test	% Change	Pre-test	Post-test	% Change
	*(206)	(195)		(108)	(100)	
1.............	85.9	81.0	−4.9	89.7	85.9	−3.8
2.............	92.7	95.9	+3.2	90.7	96.0	+5.3
3.............	69.1	67.2	−1.9	70.1	63.6	−6.5
4.............	67.5	69.6	+2.1	68.5	75.8	+7.3
5.............	90.3	89.2	−1.1	86.1	88.8	+2.7
6.............	71.2	76.0	+4.8	72.2	76.5	+4.3
7.............	91.7	89.7	−2.0	88.0	88.9	+ .9

* Denotes total number of subjects.

failed to establish any differences between the two groups at either the beginning or the end of the study with regard to the self-concept items. An individual-items analysis is presented in table 28.

INTERPERSONAL-COMPETENCE SCALE

Pre- and post-test scores on Rothstein's interpersonal-competence scale (11 items) were also compared for both experimental and control subjects. The findings indicated that, although there was no significant difference in mean scores between the two groups at the beginning and at the end of the school year, both groups showed slight but significant improvement (see table 29).

TABLE 29

MEAN SCORES ON 11 INTERPERSONAL-COMPETENCE ITEMS,
PRE- AND POST-TEST, EXPERIMENTAL AND
CONTROL SUBJECTS, 1963–64

	PRE-TEST	POST-TEST	P*
Experimentals............	6.00	6.56	.05
Controls................	5.88	6.45	.05
P.....................	NS	NS	

* Denotes level of statistical significance.

Although the mean scores revealed significant improvement within the experimental and control cohorts at the end of the school year, a more detailed item analysis proved largely negative. The most pronounced improvement within the experimental group occurred on item 7 ("I trust the judgment of my friends more often than I do my own judgment") (see table 30). The only other significant difference from pre- to post-test for the experimental group occurred on item 6 in the set of 11 interpersonal-competence items ("Even when somebody doesn't agree with me, I can usually understand his reasons for not agreeing with me"). Within the control groups, the only significant improvement occurred in the response to item 10 ("I often get into hot water because I speak or act without thinking") (see table 30).

TABLE 30

Extent of Change in the Percentage of Subjects Scoring Favorably on 11 Interpersonal-competence Items, Pre- and Post-test, 1963–64

ITEM NUMBER	EXPERIMENTALS			CONTROLS		
	Pre-test	Post-test	% Change	Pre-test	Post-test	% Change
	*(206)	(195)		(108)	(100)	
1	74.8	82.0	+ 7.2	72.2	72.4	+ .2
2	62.6	59.5	− 3.1	60.2	66.7	+ 6.5
3	67.5	72.8	+ 5.3	65.4	72.7	+ 7.3
4	71.4	72.3	+ .9	69.4	71.7	+ 2.3
5	29.1	34.4	+ 5.3	30.6	35.4	+ 4.8
6†	61.2	72.3	+11.1	55.1	64.6	+ 9.5
7†	60.2	81.2	+21.0	62.0	73.7	+11.7
8	46.1	51.3	+ 5.2	43.5	46.9	+ 3.4
9	31.1	35.6	+ 4.5	28.7	35.7	+ 7.0
10‡	32.7	39.5	+ 6.8	38.0	51.5	+13.5
11	52.4	54.4	+ 2.0	50.9	52.5	+ 1.6

* Denotes total number of subjects.
† Change in experimental group at .05 or better.
‡ Change in control group at .05 or better.

ATTITUDES TOWARD SCHOOL

The insensitivity of the abbreviated socialization, self-concept, and interpersonal-competence scales led the project's research staff to develop new scales to measure the several dimensions of school attitudes.[2] The improvement of school attitudes was clearly one of the major goals of the demonstration project. On the basis of pilot research with 148 seventh-grade boys, plus "sympathetic introspection" and a review of the literature, the research staff identified 6 theoretically separate variables, jointly comprising a generalized attitude toward school. These variables were labeled: (1) capacity to learn; (2) value of education; (3) legitimacy (of the manifest functions of the school); (4) teachers—general (interpersonal relations between teachers and pupils); (5) teachers—personal (respondent's concrete experiences with teachers); and (6) teachers—academic (the competency and commitment of teachers to their work) (see schedules in Appendixes F and G).

In order to measure these dimensions, a large number of questions were assembled and eventually reduced to a total of 89 items. These were then pretested on 97 seventh-grade boys, and the responses were subjected to Guttman scale analysis and the Scale Value Difference methods. The final schedule, after removal of the non-scalable and low SVD (scale value difference) items, contained a total of 48 items in the above 6 subscales. Using four groups of respondents, according to teacher nomination and police contact, the coefficients of reproducibility and the minimal marginal reproducibility varied only slightly. All except one of the 24 coefficients of reproducibility reached .90, which is the generally accepted cutting point. In this one instance, the coefficient at .89 was close enough to be deemed acceptable.

Before presenting the pre-test–post-test data on the experimental, control, and comparison subjects, some additional work deserves brief discussion. In evaluating these 6 dimensions of attitudes toward school, the staff used all the subjects assigned to the experimental, control, and comparison groups in the second cohort year, 1964–65. These boys were divided into the four teacher-nomination and police-contact categories as follows: known delinquents; high delinquency potential (nominated bad boys but without known police contact) ; moderate delinquency potential (nominated as *possible* and without known police contact) ; and low delinquency potential (nominated good boys—that is, as *unlikely* to get into trouble).

As expected, the greatest differences in attitudes toward school on each of the 6 dimensions were found between the known delinquents and the low-delinquency-potential group. Thus, the known delinquents were more negative on each of the subscales but very much so on 4 of the 6 of them, specifically, capacity to learn, legitimacy of school, teachers—general, and teachers—personal. Ironically, the subscales concerned with the value of education and with teachers—academic, failed to differentiate the known delinquents from the good boys. The two middle groups (those with high and with moderate delinquency potential) varied little on any of the subscales, although they responded more like the known delinquents than the nondelinquents. Nevertheless, the staff concluded: "Data show that the individual's perception of his capacity to learn, as well as other dimensions of attitude toward school, associates highly with delinquency."[3]

Attitude schedules based on the 6 Guttman subscales were administered at the beginning (pre-test) and again at the close (post-test) of the seventh-grade year on a routine basis to the 1964–65 and 1965–66 cohorts, comprising for the two years a total of 431 experimental, 347 control, and 441 good-boy comparisons. The project anticipated that the experimental students would show significantly more favorable attitudes than the controls on a pre-test–post-test basis.

This expectation that the demonstration project would be effective in modifying the generally negative attitudes of treated seventh-grade boys failed to materialize. Indeed, except on one dimension only, the 431 experimental boys were significantly more negative toward school after the program. Generally speaking, this was also the case with the controls, who were significantly less favorable on 3 of the dimensions and less favorable, though not statistically so, on 2 of the other 3 subscales. The 441 good-boy comparisons (nominated as *unlikely* to get into trouble) started and ended more favorably disposed toward school on all 6 dimensions than the bad boys (nominated by their teachers and principals as *likely* or *possible*). On 3 of the subscales, there was little pre-test–post-test change, but its direction was favorable. On another subscale there was a slight negative change. On the remaining 2 subscales, the good boys were less positive at the end.

In more specific terms, all three groups—experimentals, controls, and comparisons—were far less favorable (P ≤ .05) on the 3 subscales concerning their relationships with their teachers—general, academic, and personal—on the post- than on the pre-test. On the teachers—academic subscale, however, only the experimentals and the controls were significantly less well disposed on the post-test. On 2 of the dimensions, value of education and legitimacy of the school, the experimental subjects were significantly less positive, the controls slightly less favorable, and the good boys minimally improved at the point of post-test.

Only on one dimension, the capacity to learn, was there across-the-board improvement in all three groups. For the experimentals, the improvement was statistically significant (P ≤ .05). For the controls,

TABLE 31

PRE- AND POST-TEST MEAN SCORES ON THE 6 GUTTMAN SUBSCALES
FOR THE EXPERIMENTAL, CONTROL, AND COMPARISON SUBJECTS

SCHOOL DIMENSION*	EXPERIMENTALS	CONTROLS	COMPARISONS
Capacity to learn			
Pre-test...............	3.47	3.55	2.95
Post-test..............	3.07	3.43	2.89
P†.................	.05	NS	NS
Value of Education			
Pre-test...............	2.87	2.94	2.63
Post-test..............	3.18	2.99	2.62
P†.................	.05	NS	NS
Legitimacy of School			
Pre-test...............	2.48	2.22	1.91
Post-test..............	2.73	2.29	1.78
P†.................	.05	NS	NS
Teachers—General			
Pre-test...............	3.92	3.85	3.55
Post-test..............	4.20	4.21	3.83
P†.................	.05	.05	.05
Teachers—Personal			
Pre-test...............	2.44	2.35	1.84
Post-test..............	2.69	2.88	2.10
P†.................	.05	.05	.05
Teachers—Academic			
Pre-test...............	3.01	3.02	2.93
Post-test..............	3.36	3.22	3.04
P†.................	.05	.05	NS

* The higher the score, the less favorable the attitude.
† P denotes level of statistical significance.

there was some but not a significant gain. The smallest gain was shown by the good boys. In the post-test period, the 431 experimental boys were closer to the good boys in their perceptions of their capacity to learn than they were to the controls. These results are shown in table 31.

ATTITUDES TOWARD THE LAW

The second and most obvious objective of the project was to prevent vulnerable boys from becoming arrest statistics, from engaging in violational activities, and from earning the stigmatizing label of juvenile delinquent. Naturally, it was the hope of the program that the perceptions of inner-city boys toward the legal institutions and their agents would change from negative to positive, thereby preventing future involvement in law-violating activities.

The senior research associate on the project, attempted to develop sensitive, reliable, and valid scales to measure these perceptions.[4] The procedures, with only minor modifications, were identical to those used earlier to develop the 6 subscales dealing with attitudes toward school. Drawing on a variety of sources—experience, delinquency literature, available instruments—148 boys in 6 Youth Development (experimental) classes were asked to indicate things that they liked or disliked concerning the law, police, and courts. From their responses, 9 dimensions appeared to emerge: (1) policemen—relationship with kids; (2) policemen—legitimacy; (3) policemen—personal characteristics; (4) probation officers—relationship with kids; (5) probation officers—legitimacy; (6) juvenile courts—relationship with kids; (7) juvenile courts—legitimacy; (8) laws—relationship with kids; and (9) laws—legitimacy (see schedules in appendixes F and G).

From a pool of items, presumably tapping each of these aspects, 63 were finally chosen and administered to 102 experimental boys in the first cohort, 1963–64, toward the end of that school year. These items were balanced between favorable and unfavorable perceptions, in order to reduce systematic bias. The pilot results, incredible as it may appear, indicated that each of the items fitted the Guttman scale for which it was designed. The 9 Guttman subscales contained 5 to 9 items each, and the coefficient of reproducibility was well above the acceptable figure of .90 on every subscale. The minimal marginal reproducibility was also highly acceptable on the subscales.

In addition to the Guttman technique, every item was correlated with the total score on all 9 dimensions. No negative values were found, and only 4 individual items had low correlations, that is, $+.25$ or less. All items were therefore retained in the total scale. Finally, on the Scale Value Difference (SVD) technique, which seeks to evaluate each item in relation to the others, only 5 items failed to differentiate the high from the low scores at a statistically significant level. Again these items were retained principally because they had scaled well using the Guttman method.

As with the school attitude scale, the 1963–64 cohort of boys was divided for scale development purposes into four groups, consisting of a total of 626 boys to whom the law schedule was given. These four groups were: known delinquents, high delinquency potential, moderate delinquency potential, and low delinquency potential. An analysis of the median scores of the four groups of boys on the pre-test of the 9 subscales measuring attitudes toward the law revealed an extreme difference between the known delinquents and the good boys on every dimension—always favorable, as expected, to the good boys. Two middle groups—the high- and moderate-delinquency-potential boys—were found to be very close to one another in median scores, but closer to the known delinquents than to the good boys in median scores. The white boys in each of the four subgroups were found to be more favorable than the black boys on all 9 scales of perceptions toward the law.

The 9 subscales measuring attitudes toward the law were administered to the 1964–65 and 1965–66 experimental, control, and comparison subjects at the beginning and again at the close of the academic year, along with the 6 school dimensions discussed previously. Even more so than on the school subscales, the results on the law, police, court, and probation dimensions failed to show greater improvement for the experimentals than for the controls. These findings are presented in table 32.

On each of the law-attitude dimensions, the experimental boys were less favorable on the pre-test (high mean scores) than the control boys, and both groups of nominated potential delinquents were very much more negative than the good-boy comparisons. The identical pattern pertained on all 9 dimensions on the post-test (see table 32). However, on the post-test, the difference in mean scores between the 431 experimental and the 347 control subjects decreased whereas the differences in mean scores between the nominated bad and good boys remained approximately the same as in the pre-test. Most critical in terms of the demonstration project, the attitudes of the experimental boys toward the several aspects of the legal system did not improve at all. Instead, their attitudes either remained basically unchanged or, in fact, became more negative, and significantly so, on the eight-item "law—legitimacy" Guttman subscale.

More specifically, the experimental subjects were more negative on all but 3 of the 9 dimensions at the end of the seventh-grade (post-test) year when their exposure to the Youth Development Program ended than they had been at the beginning of the school year. On only 1 of the 9 dimensions, "law—legitimacy," was

TABLE 32

PRE- AND POST-TEST MEAN SCORES ON THE 9 GUTTMAN SUBSCALES FOR THE EXPERIMENTAL, CONTROL, AND COMPARISON SUBJECTS

DIMENSION*	EXPERIMENTALS	CONTROLS	COMPARISONS
Policemen—Relationship with kids			
Pre-test............	4.45	4.05	3.46
Post-test...........	4.59	4.51	3.78
P†	NS	.05	.05
Policemen—Legitimacy			
Pre-test............	3.85	3.53	3.22
Post-test...........	4.00	3.61	3.19
P†	NS	NS	NS
Policemen—Personal characteristics			
Pre-test............	3.33	3.06	2.85
Post-test...........	3.31	3.22	2.97
P†	NS	NS	NS
Probation officers— Relationship with kids			
Pre-test............	4.86	4.45	4.32
Post-test...........	4.80	4.64	4.45
P†	NS	NS	NS
Probation officers—Legitimacy			
Pre-test............	4.04	3.81	3.64
Post-test...........	4.06	3.90	3.71
P†	NS	NS	NS
Courts—Relationship with kids			
Pre-test............	4.70	4.25	3.92
Post-test...........	4.63	4.39	3.93
P†	NS	NS	NS
Courts—Legitimacy			
Pre-test............	2.95	2.62	2.31
Post-test...........	3.02	2.70	2.21
P†	NS	NS	NS
Laws—Relationship with kids			
Pre-test............	3.54	3.33	3.10
Post-test...........	3.58	3.45	3.14
P†	NS	NS	NS
Laws—Legitimacy			
Pre-test............	4.79	4.39	3.79
Post-test...........	5.14	4.62	4.10
P†	.05	NS	.05

* The higher the score, the less favorable the attitude.
† P denotes level of statistical significance.

there a statistically significant increase (unfavorable) in mean scores from pre- to post-test for the experimentals. The control boys were less favorable on all 9 of the law subscales at the end of the seventh grade (post-test) but significantly less so on only one. The good-boy comparisons had higher mean scores (unfavorable direction) on 7 of the 9 subscales at the post-test phase, of which only 2 differences between pre- and post-mean scores were statistically significant.

REMEDIAL-READING-PROGRAM EVALUATION

The Youth Development Project was oriented toward improving the self-concepts of the experimental subjects, removing some of their defeatism, and providing them with acceptable role models. These goals dictated the character of the program inputs. Nevertheless, it soon became evident that one of the major sources of low self-esteem and poor academic performance was reading deficiency—a problem characteristic of lower-class delinquents in the United States.[5] As indicated earlier, the experimental subjects entered our seventh-grade program with a mean reading achievement grade level of 5.7, and the controls averaged 5.5. In contrast, the good-boy comparisons entered the seventh grade with a reading achievement mean grade level of 6.7.

The results of the remedial reading efforts, described previously in some detail, were promising. The second cohort (1964–65) experimentals, as a whole, improved an average of 0.85 reading achievement grade levels, from the pre- to the post-treatment phase. The 1964–65 controls, who did not receive the remedial reading supplement, increased their reading achievement by only

TABLE 33

IMPROVEMENT IN EXPERIMENTALS AND CONTROLS
READING ACHIEVEMENT, 1964–65 COHORT

| | GRADE LEVEL | | IMPROVEMENT | P* | N† |
	6th Grade	7th Grade			
Experimentals........	5.79	6.64	0.85	.001	186
Controls.............	6.01	6.41	0.40	NS	73
Improvement........			+0.45	.001	

Source: Summarizes the findings by Nason E. Hall and Gordon P. Waldo, "Remedial Reading for the Disadvantaged," *Journal of Reading* 11, no. 2 (November 1967):87, table 3.
* Denotes level of statistical significance.
† Denotes number of subjects.

half as much, namely 0.40 grade levels (see table 33). This difference was statistically significant at the .001 level of confidence.

Although there is some room for optimism regarding the positive effect of the remedial reading program on the experimental boys, the net difference on the post-test between the treated and untreated subjects was generally small. In view of the hard data on school dropout and delinquency involvement, the reading improvement data offer very little consolation.

1. This discussion and analysis has been taken from a M.A. thesis evaluating the first year's results. See Margaret Ann Zahn, "An Evaluation of an Experimental Delinquency Prevention Program" (Master's thesis, The Ohio State University, 1964), pp. 26–39.

2. Part of this material on attitudes toward school can be found in greater detail in Nason E. Hall and Gordon P. Waldo, "School Identification and Delinquency Proneness," *Journal of Research in Crime and Delinquency* (July 1967):231–42.

3. Ibid., p. 242.

4. Part of this section summarizes the project by Gordon P. Waldo, "Boys' Perceptions of Outer Containment and Delinquency Potential" (Ph.D. diss., Ohio State University, 1967).

5. This section summarizes the findings by Nason E. Hall and Gordon P. Waldo, "Remedial Reading for the Disadvantaged," *Journal of Reading* 11, no. 2 (November 1967):81–92.

CHAPTER EIGHT

An Interview Follow-up

In addition to the assessment of attitude change toward law and the schools at the beginning and end of the demonstration program year, a concerted effort was also made to interview in depth available and cooperating boys from the experimental and control groups of the second cohort (1964–65) two years after the seventh grade. This chapter is concerned with the results of the interview follow-up.

In May and June of 1967, three of the four original project teachers interviewed samples of experimentals and controls from the second (1964–65) cohort year. At the time of the follow-up interview, most of the subjects were just finishing the ninth grade. The purpose of the follow-up interview was to assess the progress of the boys in each of the two groups, to determine whether differences existed between them with regard to such qualities as appearance, demeanor, extracurricular interests, and self-reported misbehavior (see the interview schedule in Appendix H).

Most of the interviews, especially those with the controls, were conducted after school at the schools the boys were attending. A few were conducted in the boys' homes. The boys were, in all cases, interviewed individually. All three teachers were working full time during regular school hours but conducted the interviews on their own time after school.

Interviews were obtained from 120 out of 219 experimentals (55%) and 42 out of 123 controls (34%) in the second cohort (1964–65). No attempt was made to locate and interview all of the experimentals and controls because such a task would have required much more time and resources than were available. For the same reason, no attempt was made to sample any of the good-boy comparisons. Instead, the three teachers sought out all the 1964–65 experimentals and controls they could find in the respective schools in which they had taught the special seventh-grade project classes. They also jointly sought out bad boys in the two schools in which the fourth project teacher (who was not involved in the follow-up interviewing) had taught.

The boys who were not contacted and, therefore, not interviewed included those who had either dropped out of school, moved out of the Columbus area, been incarcerated, refused to be interviewed (mostly controls who did not know the teachers from classroom experience), or were simply too difficult to locate. Lack of time was an added limitation, inasmuch as it was necessary to have the interviewing completed by the end of June, 1967. Those who had moved away and those who could not be located and interviewed within the allotted time comprised a large proportion of those not sampled. Since the teachers were paid for each interview, they naturally tried to get as many as they could.

Regrettably, this interviewing procedure was biased in favor of those in school, those who knew the three teachers, and probably also those who were positive in their attitudes toward the Youth Development Program and toward the post-program interview. To determine the extent of this bias, the follow-up experimental and control subjects were compared with the non-interviewed experimental and control boys. The general unrepresentativeness of both the experimental and control interview samples, particularly the former, is shown in the comparative data presented in Appendix I.

INTERVIEW RESULTS

The interview schedule, contained in Appendix H, consisted of three separate parts. The first section called for the subjective evaluation of the interviewees' appearance, demeanor, and future prospects. The second part of the interview schedule attempted to assess the boys' perception, feelings, and intentions concerning school, after-school activities, and friendships. For the experimental respondents of the second cohort (1964–65) only, there were several questions about the Youth Development Project program, its value to the boys themselves, and the advisability of extending it to all seventh-grade pupils. This entire section called for structured answers, but it also provided the interviewee or respondent an opportunity for in-depth discussion. The last part of the schedule contained 33 items of self-reported behavior. Included in this list were 6 items of the Nye-Short Scale of misconduct, 15 additional questions eliciting self-reported misdeeds, and, by contrast, 12 items in which positive (good) behaviors were assessed. The scoring was such that the lower the total, the more favorable the behavior; the higher the total, the greater the self-reported misconduct.

INTERVIEWER RATINGS

As already noted, the project teacher-interviewers were asked to evaluate subjectively the contacted experimental and control boys on 10 items in three areas —appearance, demeanor, and future prospects. The results indicate that the teachers thought the experimentals were doing considerably better than the controls on most of the specific items.

Appearance

There were no significant differences between the ratings of experimental (treated) and control (untreated) interviewed boys on 2 of the 3 appearance items (neatness and cleanliness) (see Appendix H). In regard to the third appearance item, health, a significantly greater percentage of the experimentals than of the controls were rated as being in good health.

Demeanor

The project teacher-interviewers rated each of the experimental and control follow-up boys on 4 behavioral characteristics: cooperativeness, ease and comfort in the interview setting, honesty in response, and a general assessment of delinquency potential. Ratings on all 4 items were significantly more favorable for the experimentals and overwhelmingly so on the delinquency assessment (see table 34).

TABLE 34

PERCENTAGES OF EXPERIMENTAL AND CONTROL FOLLOW-UP BOYS
AS RATED BY THE INTERVIEWERS ON DEMEANOR

DEMEANOR	EXPERIMENTALS	CONTROLS	P*
Cooperative...............	88.8	57.1	.001
Comfortable...............	83.4	52.4	.001
Honest...................	79.3	60.0	.05
Delinquency assessment			
Nondelinquent...........	61.7	22.5	
Unsure.................	24.4	50.0	.001
Delinquent..............	13.9	27.5	

* Denotes level of statistical significance based on chi square analysis.

It is interesting to compare these follow-up assess-
ments, made at the end of the ninth grade, with the
actual outcome of the same boys at the end of the tenth
grade. By this time, despite the teacher-interviewer
ratings above, the percentages of the interviewed boys
with police contacts in the post-program period was
greater for the experimentals, but only very slightly.
Similarly, the known violations committed by the interviewed boys at any time in their lives, were only
slightly greater for the experimentals. According to
the teacher-interviewers, 61.7% of their former project student respondents were nondelinquent (see table
34). This was almost precisely the official situation for
these boys by the end of the tenth grade. On the other
hand, the teachers, knowing the controls only inci-
dentally, if at all, hedged their predictions on them.
Fully half were labeled as *possible* by the teacher-
interviewers. Most of these boys, as it turned out, remained free from police contact throughout. If nothing
else, then, knowing the boys well resulted in accurate
prediction; lack of familiarity, in hedging in favor of
delinquency.

Future Prediction

The former project teacher-interviewers also rated the interviewees in terms of likelihood of their completing high school, getting into trouble with the police, and making a good family adjustment. On the first two variables, the experimentals were rated superior to the controls. On the family variable, no difference was found (see table 35).

TABLE 35

PERCENTAGES OF EXPERIMENTAL AND CONTROL FOLLOW-UP BOYS
AS RATED BY THE INTERVIEWERS ON FUTURE PROSPECTS

FUTURE PREDICTIONS	EXPERIMENTALS	CONTROLS	P*
High school			
Finish...................	52.9	33.3	
Unsure..................	37.0	45.2	.05
Dropout.................	10.1	21.4	
Police involvement			
No trouble...............	58.5	26.2	
Unsure..................	29.7	45.2	.001
Trouble.................	11.9	28.6	
Family adjustment			
Good...................	54.9	40.6	
Fair....................	33.6	40.6	NS
Poor...................	11.5	18.8	

* Denotes level of statistical significance based on chi square analysis.

Here again, the teacher-interviewers tended more frequently to rate the contacted experimentals favorable whereas their evaluations of the contacted controls were more frequently listed as unsure. The teacher-interviewers ratings were, in fact, quite correct on the experimentals. For example, only 11.7% had dropped out of school by the end of the tenth grade. The teacher-interviewers, not knowing the contacted controls as well, underrated their potential for finishing school and overrated their "goodness." It is the opinion of the investigators that because the teacher-interviewers did not maintain the same close contact with the families as with many of the boys themselves, they tended to even out their ratings of the cohesiveness of the families of the contacted experimental and control boys (see table 35).

BOYS' PERCEPTIONS

During the course of the interview, the follow-up boys were questioned in some detail about various aspects of school, parental relationships, and after-school and summer work. However, this intensive interviewing yielded no major differences between the experimental and control interviewees.

School Assessment

As will be noticed in Appendix H, 9 items concerning school were included in the schedule. In addition to questioning on a yes-no, like-dislike, or similar basis, the teacher-interviewers tried to probe for more detail. Most of the responses obtained were conventional and not rewarding with regard to permitting a better understanding of the interviewees' views of the world. The responses suggest resignation with regard to all aspects of school rather than either positive affirmation or outright rejection. To the question, "How do you like school?", about half of all respondents replied, "It's okay." About 38% liked it, and the remainder expressed genuine dislike. Of those who were positive toward school, most of the respondents (experimentals as well as controls) saw it as necessary and valuable for the future and also as a chance to learn. For a few, school was fun; and for another small minority of the respondents, school provided the opportunity to participate in sports. For one student—perhaps an honest reflection of our turbulent times—school was a place where kids are equal. No differences were observed between the experimentals and controls regarding their assessment of school.

Three questions in the schedule (see Appendix H) dealt with the rating of English, mathematics, and all other teachers, as easy or hard to get along with. On none of these ratings was there any significant difference between the two follow-up groups (experimentals and controls). About 83% of all the boys interviewed rated their English teachers (eighth grade) as easy to get along with; a slightly higher percentage thought the mathematics teachers were easy to relate to; and a similar percentage was found with regard to all other teachers considered together. Apart from answering whether a teacher was easy or hard to interact with, only about 30 respondents gave reasons for their answers. But from these, it appeared obvious that a teacher was rated "easy" if he or she presented no special problems to the boy or was somewhat helpful. Teachers were rated as hard to get along with when the student felt interpersonal distance or when the teacher was seen as too strict.

That our follow-up interviewees were at times troublesome in school is evident from their responses to the next two questions. To our question, "Have you been sent to the office since the beginning of the new school semester in February (our interviewing was done in May and June) because of being in trouble?", 67.2% of the experimentals and 63.4% of the controls replied in the affirmative. The reasons for this action, as stated by the boys, were as follows: cutting class, messing around, fighting, threatening or talking back to a teacher, talking in class, acting up in class, nonparticipation, arguing and swearing in class, poor appearance, smoking, chewing gum, carrying a weapon, fooling around with girls, drinking, general obstreperousness, loitering, theft, and other activities ranging from the incidental and mischievous to the serious and harmful (fighting with a knife). One wonders, after examining these replies, how the junior high schools in which these boys were students were able to function and to provide an atmosphere conducive to learning. Are these difficult and disruptive boys merely biding their time until age 16 when they can legally leave school, or is it the school that produces this discontent; or is it both? Since these were the positively self-selected of our original treated and nontreated groups, how much more serious are the problems presented by those not interviewed? How much more disruptive could they be?

Although nearly two-thirds of the follow-up boys reported being sent to the principal's office for the various infractions noted above, only about a third admitted absenting themselves from school during the second semester of the eighth grade. As to what they did on the days they were truant, the responses indicated that most simply stayed in and around home and "messed around," played cards, or went for a ride (one boy in a car he stole for the occasion). There were no differences between the experimentals and controls in the percentage who truanted or, from what we could gather from their accounts, in their activities while truant.

The last school item concerned plans and prospects for going to high school. Seven possibilities were offered the interviewees: going to high school with a very good chance of finishing; going with a fair chance of finishing; going with a poor chance of finishing; not going but getting a job; not going but "messing around"; not going but with indefinite plans; and not going but with no specification as to future plans. The results of the analysis of responses to these 7 choices vary with the nature of the combination of responses. Thus, about 90% said that they will go on to high school and will have, by their own estimates, a very good or fair chance of finishing. Less than half, however, thought their chances of finishing high school were very good (49.2% of the experimentals and 34.2% of the controls). See table 36 for a tabulation of the above findings.

After-School Involvement

Three items in the schedule (see Appendix H) pertained to after-school involvement with the law during the semester then nearly ended. Without going into excessive detail, 11.9% and 19.1% of the experimentals and controls, respectively, indicated that they had experienced trouble with the law after school. This is really a very high incidence rate for less than half a year, although the nature of the involvement was very often, but not always, minor, with such offenses as fighting, auto theft (joy riding), shoplifting, and curfew violations predominating.

Nearly all of the interviewed boys reported that they went out after supper and, indeed, most of their police contacts occurred in the evening. Again, the experi-

TABLE 36

PERCENTAGE OF INTERVIEWED EXPERIMENTAL AND CONTROL SUBJECTS
RESPONDING TO STRUCTURED QUESTIONS ON SCHOOL

SCHOOL VARIABLES	EXPERIMENTALS	CONTROLS	P*
General attitude toward school			
Like it....................	37.3	42.9	
It's OK...................	54.2	50.0	NS
Dislike it................	8.5	7.1	
English teacher			
Easy to get along with......	83.8	83.3	
Hard to get along with......	16.2	16.7	NS
Mathematics teacher			
Easy to get along with.......	89.1	83.3	NS
Hard to get along with......	10.9	16.7	
Other teachers			
Easy to get along with......	87.6	78.4	NS
Hard to get along with......	12.4	21.6	
Been sent to the principal's office			
Yes......................	67.2	63.4	NS
No.......................	32.8	36.6	
Been truant			
Yes......................	28.6	39.0	NS
No.......................	71.4	61.0	
Intend to go to high school			
Yes, and very good chance to finish.	49.2	34.2	
Yes, and fair chance to finish	43.2	51.2	NS
No	7.6	14.6	

* Denotes level of statistical significance based on chi square analysis.

mentals and controls differed little in their responses
to these items.

Jobs

Two items on the schedule pertained to job status,
full- or part-time, during the summers following both
the seventh and eighth grades. Of the followed-up experimental subjects, 51.3% reported a job of some sort
during the summer following the seventh grade; 59.0%

reported employment during the last previous summer, following the eighth grade. The respective percentages for the controls were 57.1 and 51.2. These minor differences were neither statistically significant nor especially revealing. The reported jobs were mostly of the unskilled variety and included newspaper delivery boy, lawnmowing work, store clerk, manual labor in construction, and service jobs of various types.

The most impressive aspect of these questions was in pointing up the paucity of meaningful and remunerative employment opportunities available to inner-city boys in junior high school. Certainly any program designed to provide summer employment would have met with the approval of our interviewees. Regrettably, modern industrial organization is especially hard on the young, the unskilled, and the inexperienced; and our interviewees met all these criteria. That so many inner-city boys are idle each summer is hardly of benefit to anyone, least of all to the police.

Clubs, Teams, and Honors

One item in the follow-up schedule pertained to membership and participation in clubs or on teams, plus the receipt of honors. Interestingly, it was one of the few questions that differentiated the experimentals and controls at a statistically significant level of confidence. Some 47.5% of the experimental interviewees and 26.8% of the controls were involved in some school or after-school activities.

The range of involvement was surprisingly wide. For both groups, the largest participation was in sports. Two experimental boys received awards for sports, and several others were members of a sports club. Hi-Y membership was second in importance, numerically at least, and a surprising number of the experimental boys reported being members of the Sea Cadets, Boy Scouts, church clubs, boys' clubs, recreation centers, and other clubs. Most impressive was the academic participation of the experimentals. There were honor-roll members (2) ; citizenship-awards recipients (7) ; student-council members (3) ; student-newspaper workers (2) ; chess, speech, dramatics, French, science, and model-builders' club members; band, orchestra, and choir members; and audio-visual aides, hall monitors, bookroom helpers, and guidance-officer helpers. One student received an award for his art work. This panoply of activities is most encouraging and does much to account for the noncontact boys among the followed-up experimentals and controls.

In contrast, the interviewees who said they were not involved in clubs or teams specified the following major reasons for their nonparticipation: disinterest, no time, dislike activities, too old, friends won't participate, hate school, and not smart enough (a most pathetic self-image). A few disliked the school coach or the club leader, and some others had tried but failed to make a team.

Interpersonal Relations

A comparison of four items in the follow-up with the same four presented in the seventh-grade interview revealed that in the areas of interpersonal relationships with parents or parent surrogates, siblings, other adults in the family, and young relatives, there was no greater improvement or deterioration in the interactional patterns of the experimentals than of the controls. These items posed a problem because a large number of the follow-up boys came from non-intact families. For example, only 81 (67.5%) experimental boys responded with regard to their fathers whereas 118 (98.3%) answered about their relationships with their mothers. Out of the 42 controls, 28 (66.7%) responded about their fathers, and all 42 (100%) about their mothers. In general, relationships with the fathers appeared to have improved markedly in the interim since the seventh grade in both groups of respondents.

The follow-up subjects were much more laudatory about their mothers than their fathers. Most of the respondents said they got along well with their mothers, felt that they were understood by them, and felt trusted by them. With regard to their relationships with their siblings, the responding experimentals and controls indicated they were now generally more favorable to their brothers and their sisters than when they were in the seventh grade (two years earlier). The same attitude also prevailed toward other adults, such as grandparents, aunts and uncles, and guardians.

SELF-REPORTED BEHAVIOR

Thirty-three questions were included in a special follow-up interview schedule, administered at the same time as the schedule in Appendix H, to elicit self-reported misconduct (see Appendix J). These 33 questions covered 19 items taken from Nye-Short, 6 of which (designated below as N-S items) are items that have been found to form a Guttman scale. The remainder were drawn from other self-report instruments and varied in directionality. The "bad" items indicated a negative activity; the "good" items, a positive or counterdelinquent activity. The starred items were the ones found to correlate most highly with the total score. These 17 starred, or significant, items were derived using the arbitrary criterion that an item would be included if it correlated with the total score at +.40 or higher and conjointly had a Fisher t coefficient of at least 6.0. In looking at these items (see Appendix J), it might be helpful to note that the item with the highest correlation was question 22 (+.65) followed by numbers 25 (+.60), 17 (+.58), 28 (+.55), 3 (+.54), 12 (+.54), 16 (+.54), 15 (+.52), 20 (+.49), 10 (+.46), 13 (+.45), 23 (+.45), 26 (+.45), 1 (+.44), 27 (+.43), and 30 (+.43). The item with the lowest correlation was 21 (+.01). Eight others correlated in the +.20 to +.29 range and the remainder in the +.30 to +.40 range.

The results of the analysis of this self-reporting instrument are most interesting. There are three general findings. First, using mean scores to analyze all 33 items—the bad items, the good items, and the Nye-Short–scaled items—the experimental and control follow-up interviewees did not differ significantly from each other. In terms of direction, however, the experimentals scored more favorably (less self-reported misconduct) on all four measures (see table 37).

TABLE 37

MEAN SCORES OF SELF-REPORTED MISCONDUCT BY EXPERIMENTAL
AND CONTROL FOLLOW-UP INTERVIEWEES

SELF-REPORT*	EXPERIMENTALS	CONTROLS	P†
All items	29.15	31.02	NS
"Bad" items	13.93	15.67	NS
"Good" items	15.22	15.36	NS
Nye-Short scaled items	4.57	5.55	NS

* The lower the score the less the self-reported misconduct.
† Denotes level of statistical significance; based on critical ratio of the difference between means.

As an indication of the extent of participation in illegal or deviant activities, the most significant items (17 in number) were examined individually. On each of the 17, fewer experimentals than controls admitted misconduct (P = .001, using a sign test) (see table 38). Whether these self-reports reflect the reality or merely the greater sophistication of the treated respondents (for which our program may itself have been responsible) is a provocative issue. The percentages in table 38 always indicate the fa-

TABLE 38

PERCENTAGE OF EXPERIMENTALS AND CONTROLS WHO RESPONDED
FAVORABLY (NEVER OR VERY OFTEN) ON 17
SELF-REPORTED ITEMS

	EXPERIMENTALS	CONTROLS
Driving a car without a license or permit*	40.8	35.7
Truanted from school*	47.5	40.4
Refused to smoke†	37.5	30.9
Been placed on school probation or suspended*	58.3	52.4
Defied parental authority*	59.2	54.7
Driven a car recklessly*	74.2	73.8
Taken little things (worth less than $2)*	41.7	26.2
Taken things of medium value (between $2 and $50)*	78.3	66.7
Taken things of large value (over $50)*. .	85.9	83.3
Taken part in gang fights*	63.3	57.2
Taken a car without the owner's knowledge*	75.8	64.3
Beat up innocent kids*	80.8	71.4
Bought or drunk beer, wine, or liquor (include at home)*	41.7	35.7
Inflicted pain on someone just to see him squirm*	75.8	66.7
Studied really hard for school†	26.6	19.0
Purposely damaged or destroyed public or private property*	58.3	52.4
Been really nice to one of your teachers†	25.00	21.4

* Indicates a response of never.
† Indicates a response of very often.

vorable response. On 14 of the 17 items, the favorable response is "never." On the other 3 items (refused to smoke, studied really hard, and been really nice to one of the teachers) the response of "very often" is the positive or favorable one.

Followed-up white boys, whether experimental or control, reported significantly more previous misconduct than the followed-up black respondents (see table 39). This pattern was consistent for the mean scores

TABLE 39

MEAN SCORES OF SELF-REPORTED MISCONDUCT OF
WHITE AND BLACK FOLLOW-UP INTERVIEWEES

SELF-REPORT*	WHITE	BLACK	P†
All items	33.46	27.07	.001
"Bad" items	16.74	12.80	.01
"Good" items.	16.72	14.27	.01
Nye-Short scaled items	5.97	4.05	.001

* The lower the score, the less the self-reported misconduct.
† Denotes level of statistical significance; based on critical ratio of the difference between means.

on all 33 self-reported items as well as on the good, bad, and Nye-Short–scaled items.

The self-reporting behavior of the followed-up boys stands in sharp contrast to their official records of police contact. As noted earlier, the black boys in the total study (all three cohorts) had significantly greater official contact than the white boys. The reversal at the point of follow-up interview with the second cohort may be interpreted in several ways: whites, in fact, were more involved but were less often complained about, reported, and recorded for their violations; black boys appeared more suspicious and consequently underreported on their own misconduct on the self-administered checklist; certain of the activities on the self-report instrument (defied parental authority, for example) were less applicable to black students; and finally, the white students tended to respond dichotomously (never or very often), whereas the black students were more likely to choose a response intermediate between these extremes. There are, of course, still other alternative explanations but little concrete support for any of them.

As shown in table 40, the black interviewees re-

TABLE 40

PERCENTAGE OF WHITE AND BLACK EXPERIMENTALS AND CONTROLS
WHO RESPONDED FAVORABLY (NEVER OR VERY OFTEN)
ON 17 SELF-REPORTED ITEMS

	EXPERIMENTALS		CONTROLS	
	White	Black	White	Black
Driven a car without a license or permit*...............	38.3	42.5	27.8	41.7
Truanted from school*...........	38.3	53.4	27.8	50.0
Refused to smoke†...............	31.9	41.1	16.7	41.7
Been placed on school probation or suspended*.................	55.3	60.3	55.6	50.0
Defied parental authority*.........	42.6	69.9	11.1	87.5
Driven a car recklessly*..........	61.7	82.2	61.1	83.3
Taken little things (worth less than $2)*....................	31.9	47.9	16.7	33.3
Taken things of medium value (between $2 and $50)*.........	72.3	82.2	38.9	87.5
Taken things of large value (over $50)*...................	83.0	87.7	66.7	95.8
Taken part in gang fights*.........	55.3	68.5	50.0	62.5
Taken a car without the owner's knowledge*...................	70.2	79.5	50.0	75.0
Beat up on innocent kids*.........	78.7	82.2	77.8	66.7
Bought or drunk beer, wine, or liquor (include at home)*.......	29.8	49.3	5.6	58.3
Inflicted pain on someone just to see him squirm*...............	74.5	76.7	61.1	70.8
Studied really hard for school†.....	23.4	28.8	11.1	25.0
Purposely damaged or destroyed public or private property*......	48.9	64.4	33.3	66.7
Been really nice to one of your teachers†....................	19.1	28.8	11.1	29.2

* Indicates a response of never.
† Indicates a response of very often.

ported less misbehavior on every comparison in the experimental group and on 15 of the 17 comparisons in the control group. Some of the percentage differences were enormous. For example, on the question concerning the use of alcohol, 29.8% of the white experimentals and 5.6% of the white controls said "never," compared with 49.3% and 58.3% respectively of the black experimentals and controls. On the question that dealt with defying parental authority, 42.6% of the white experimentals and 11.1% of the white controls said "never," contrasted with 69.9% of the black experimentals and 87.5% of the black controls. Less spectacular differences, all in the same direction however, were the characteristic of the white-black responses to the remaining 15 self-reported items.

To summarize table 40, white controls admitted more deviant, disruptive, or violational behavior than white experimentals; black controls and experimentals did not differ in their self-reports; blacks were less likely to admit violations than whites; and experimentals indicated less involvement than the controls. Conversely, in terms of self-reported noninvolvement in misconduct, the gradient was as follows: control blacks, experimental blacks, experimental whites, and control whites.

BOYS' PERCEPTIONS OF THE YOUTH DEVELOPMENT PROJECT

It is particularly fitting to conclude this chapter with the interviewed experimental boys' own evaluations of the merits and weaknesses of the Youth Development Project during the seventh grade. Four questions were asked the experimental subjects concerning the program. These were:

1. Are you glad you had this different kind of seventh-grade class?

2. Do you feel that any of the fellows you hang around with could have benefited from this kind of class?

3. Do you feel this kind of class would be good for all seventh-grade boys?

4. Would you recommend it for seventh-grade boys and girls together?

The response to the first question was overwhelmingly favorable. Nearly 97% of the boys who answered (111 of 115) were glad they had been part of our seventh-grade project class. Their subjective evaluations included the following comments: liked the curriculum materials (28); liked the field trips (28); the class was fun (25); learned more than other seventh-graders (23); liked the all-boy class (16); came to understand people better (13); learned about people and the world (9); liked the boys in the class (9); the class was easy (9), interesting (7), helped me (7), and did more for me than other classes (7); was made different (better) than other classes (7); was the best class was fun (25); learned more than other seventh teacher, liked him and received attention from him (5). There were other and less frequent answers.

Of the 4 boys who expressed negative feelings about the class, 2 disliked some of their classmates, 1 disliked the teacher, and 1 saw the self-contained classroom as being too much like elementary school. Finally, 5 of the followed-up experimentals were unwilling to make any judgments, positive or negative, regarding the Youth Development Program.

As to whether their present friends might have benefited from a seventh-grade program such as ours, 109 experimentals responded, and of these over 85% answered in the affirmative. Their reasons were much the same as those given in response to the preceding question. The benefits of the program were again enumerated in some detail, including responses such as the following: their friends would have learned to adjust better, to behave better, to understand people, to think more clearly, and to learn some useful and important things. The 16 boys who felt their friends would not have gained anything from such a class were also quite perceptive. Nine of the 16 said that by the time they reached seventh grade their friends were already bad, and, clearly, the seventh-grade Youth Development Program would have been too late for them. Two said their friends were good boys and did not need the program. The rest expressed a variety of negative views.

With regard to the extension of the project to include all seventh-grade boys, 92 (81.4%) of the 113 followed-up experimental boys thought the idea had merit. Their answers again indicated respect for the program and approval of the curriculum, project teachers, and classroom decorum and functioning. Those objecting to its extension focused their responses around the theme that most seventh-grade boys did not require such a program.

Finally, over three-quarters of the interviewed former-experimental subjects indicated that they would be opposed to the inclusion of coeds in the self-contained project classes. Their disapproval was expressed in these terms: having girls in the class would make it harder to express oneself freely and openly (44) ; girls like different things (12) ; the boys would mess around more (7) ; girls have different problems, act silly, and don't need the specialized curriculum; and the teacher would favor the girls.

Measured, then, by the retrospective evaluation of the former experimental boys themselves, as well as the teachers appraisals discussed earlier in this chapter, the Youth Development Project had a positive impact. Unfortunately, this favorable impact could not be documented by the hard data obtained from police and school records.

CHAPTER NINE

Summary and Conclusions

The present monograph presents an assessment of an experimental in-school delinquency prevention program. The experimental program was conducted in the seventh grade of all inner-city junior high schools in Columbus, Ohio, during three school years. The experimental and control subjects (boys) had been nominated by their sixth-grade teachers and their elementary school principals as headed for trouble with the law; the good-boy comparisons, as not headed for trouble. In all, 1,726 boys—experimental, control, and comparison—were followed for four consecutive yearly periods—at the end of the seventh, eighth, ninth, and tenth grades—to assess the outcome of the prevention program.

In a broader context, this monograph represents the culmination of fifteen years of systematic research on the role of the self-concept in the identification, prevention, and control of juvenile delinquency. The investi-

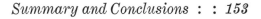

gators began with the knowledge that even in the most highly delinquent, economically deprived, and socially disorganized areas of our major cities, most boys grow to manhood and to blue collar, working-class status without significant officially acted-upon delinquency involvement.

A varied and seemingly inexhaustible supply of data was accumulated on each of the 1,726 subjects of the study. This information included three time periods: before the seventh grade, during the seventh grade, and three years after the seventh grade. When these data were reduced, rotated, and analyzed the following results became evident:

1. On none of the outcome variables were the experimental subjects significantly different from the controls. This was especially and most painfully evident in the school-performance and police-contact data. There were no significant differences in the number of boys who experienced contact with the police, the frequency of such contact, or the seriousness of the unreported behavior. In regard to the school data, the dropout rate, attendance, grades, and school-achievement levels of all three groups of boys were very much alike.

2. The police involvement of both the experimentals and controls increased with age as did the seriousness of the offenses. By the end of the tenth grade approximately 47% of all nominated bad boys (experimentals as well as controls) had become known to the police; mostly, however, for relatively minor violations of municipal ordinances or commonplace misdemeanors.

3. The school performance of the experimentals and controls deteriorated with age. This was evident in attendance, dropout, and school grades.

4. Racial differences were highly significant in the areas of criminal-involvement and school-performance variables. On both counts, the white subjects in the experimental and control groups fared better than their black counterparts.

5. Although the same trends toward greater delinquency involvement and poorer school performance with age characterized the good-boy comparison group, these boys continued to maintain their superiority on these measures in every time period: before the seventh grade, during the seventh grade, and three years thereafter. This finding provides additional confirmation for our general thesis concerning the relative insulation of good boys in high-delinquency areas.

6. The findings on the attitudinal dimensions paralleled those on the behavioral data. In the first cohort (1963–64), no significant attitude change was observed at the end of the seventh grade when compared with the end of the sixth-grade. When improvement did occur on the tests (the Socialization and self-concept scales) used on the first cohort (1963–64), it was no greater for the experimental than for the control subjects. The improvement could be attributed, in most part, to the test-retest learning situation rather than to genuine alterations in self-perceptions and other perceptions.

7. Similarly, despite the rigorousness of the methods used in developing 9 Guttman-type subscales on perceptions of law, police, and courts and 6 Guttman subscales on school, teacher, and educational dimensions, no marked differences were found between the pre- and post-program responses of the experimental and control subjects tested in the second (1964–65) and the third (1965–66) cohorts.

8. Personal interviews were conducted, whenever possible, with former experimental and control subjects of the 1964–65 cohort in the spring of 1967. According to the teacher-interviewers, the experimental boys were doing very much better than their control counterparts. This was particularly evident in the section on demeanor, which included cooperativeness, ease of interaction, honesty, and delinquency assessment. In all these respects, the teachers were more impressed with the followed-up experimental boys than with the followed-up control boys. The teacher-interviewers also were confident that fewer of the followed-up experimentals than control interviewees would become school dropouts or "police blotter" statistics. In short, and not at all unexpectedly or unwelcome, the three project teacher-interviewers were impressed by the positive gains made by their former charges in comparison with the controls. Unfortunately, the hard data do not reflect this improvement or optimism. The attitude responses noted above and the answers to the specific interview questions covering progress in school, after-school activities, interpersonal relationships, and self-reported misconduct likewise do not reflect the optimism of the project teachers concerning the greater improvement of the experimental boys. In general, however, the experimental boys did respond slightly more favorably, but certainly not to the point of statistical significance.

9. Last, when questioned about their reactions to the Youth Development program in the seventh grade, the interviewed experimental subjects were overwhelmingly favorable to the program. They were pleased to have been in this special type of class and thought that many of their friends could have benefited

from it and that it merited extension to include all seventh-grade boys in the school. This enthusiasm for the program, like that of the teachers, was impressive. Still, it would have been more impressive if this indication of favorable impact could have been translated into behavioral terms, such as better school performance and fewer police contacts.

POSSIBLE EXPLANATIONS FOR FAILURE

In judging the failure of the project from the standpoint of recorded police contacts and school-performance data, one could justifiably contend that the "medicine" (the feed-in to the experimental predelinquents) was not strong enough. As will be remembered, the preventive "medicine" of the project consisted of the following ingredients:

1. An all-boy seventh-grade class of 25 to 30 boys meeting for three class hours in succession with the same teacher, called a self-contained class. (All seventh-grade classes in Columbus, Ohio, schools at the time of the project operated self-contained classes.)

2. Interspersed with the required classroom diet of world geography, social studies, and Ohio history was the role-model supplement, activating interactional discussion.

3. The role-model lesson plans that were developed for this program were organized around five themes: the world of work, the world of school, the world of government, the world of the family, and getting along with others.

4. The project teachers, who were specially pre-

pared and instructed by daily after-school seminars, made as uniform a presentation of material and handled the classes in as uniform a manner as was possible to achieve.

5. The project teachers were trained to play the role of the "significant other" to the boys of their self-contained classes.

6. Classroom discipline was based on an agreed-upon method, which was called "respecting the rights of others." According to this approach, no boy was sent to the principal's office for discipline matters. He was nodded to, left the room, and sat in front of the classroom door until he felt ready to return and respect the rights of others.

7. If any boy in the project class raised the question as to why he was selected for this class, he was told the teacher wanted him.

The theory behind the approach of the project was that the inner-city boy at the threshold of adolescence needed to internalize models of behavior and perceptions of self that could build up some inner self-control, which in turn could withstand the "happenstances" of his family, neighborhood, and companions.

The project also assumed that the sixth-grade teachers in the schools that fed the junior high schools had a good sense of the way their boys were headed—that they could predict those headed for trouble and those not headed for trouble, just as the country doctor or the family physician years ago could sense directionality of growth in children of his patients.

It appears that the sixth-grade teachers were not as good prognosticators of directionality of sixth-grade boys as the principal and coprincipal investigators of the project had assumed. There is some likelihood that the results of the project might have been somewhat more positive in determining less police contacts and better school performance if the boys selected for the experimental project had been more definitely predelinquent subjects. If and when a similar project in the future needs to determine more accurately who is headed and not headed for delinquency at the threshold of adolescence, a valid pencil-and-paper test of directionality might be available.

There is reason to suspect that the exposure to role-model internalization was not intensive enough (that is, did not reach the inner self). Maybe, the interaction generated by the discussion of role-model lesson plans was not dramatic or pervasive enough to get inside the youth. Perhaps the exposure to role models that the project presented to the experimental boys was not extensive enough. More time devoted to such presentation in self-contained classes might have had a more decisive impact. As it was, the project teachers had to find ways to infuse the role-model material into classroom presentation by speeding up the presentation of the required coverage (that is, world geography, Ohio history, and social studies).

The role-model lesson plans could have lacked significance for 13-year-old inner-city boys. The lesson plans may have been off target, and more effective models, capable of being internalized and vaccinating the self against deviance, might have been used. Maybe the project should have experimented with the kinds of models inner-city boys can readily internalize. Perhaps the project's models were too middle class to be convincing to inner-city boys, although the staff tried to overcome a middle-class stance. For example, in one lesson plan, the boys were asked to find out about the best worker on their city block; talk to others about this person and talk to him personally; then, come to class and be ready to put his characteristics on the blackboard. Nevertheless, it is undoubtedly difficult to present role models to inner-city youths of America without exuding a bias of middle-class values.

The above comments are concerned with the probable shortcomings of the program, both in content and in presentation. There are undoubtedly basic shortcomings, independent of the limitations of content and its delivery, that are related to measurement of outcome, directionality of behavior, and behavioral change over time. One should remember that the latter set of limitations plagues the entire field of measurement of outcome and behavioral change. What takes place during "treatment," institutionalization, or participation in a program designed or assumed to bring about positive changes in approach to life, in attitudes, in life style, in self-perceptions, and so forth?

Unfortunately, in the field of crime and delinquency, the most available criterion for outcome—success or failure—of any program for handling offenders or for preventing delinquency has been the recorded official involvement of the "clients" with the caretakers of society (truant officers, police, court officers, probation officers, parole officers, and victims and observers who complain to the police). For example, the criterion of success or failure of probation has been whether, during the period of official supervision, the probationer has been cited to appear before the court for violating the rules of probation or whether the probationer has been arrested by the police for another offense. In the instance of parole, success or failure is judged by whether the parolee is returned to prison for violating the rules of parole or is arrested for a new offense. In some studies, outcome of probation or of parole is judged by whether the former "client" has or has not been arrested or convicted of another offense one year after the termination of his probation or his parole.

It has become increasingly evident to researchers in the field that failure, as judged by reported violations of rules by a caretaker officer or by arrest for a new offense, depends on the decision of the caretaker (probation or parole officer) or of the police officer to take action. In the instance of arrests, there is often a preliminary decision on the part of the victim or observer of the offense to complain to the police. In other words, the outcome as judged by reported violations of rules or by reported arrests is almost an unmanageable variable as a measure of outcome.

This is less true in instances of school truancy, which is recorded as truancy and acted upon by attendance officers or by visiting teachers. The *number* of absences is not the matter of decision on the part of the caretaker, but taking action on so many unexcused absences *is* a matter of decision. Even grades in school are not really objective criteria of performance and are likely to represent decisions or judgments on the part of the teachers.

Unfortunately, follow-up studies of "treatment" and "prevention" have had very little alternative besides using the so-called hard data of records of action taken in individual cases, which largely represent the variations in the decision-making process of the caretakers —to take action or not to take action.

THE NEED FOR NEW MEASURING DEVICES

It should be possible in the not-too-distant future to discover appropriate measures of the impact of a treatment or prevention program on the person or to discover appropriate measures of the behavioral changes that have taken place in the person by virtue of his participation in a program. One way of doing this would be to develop certain "before and after" tests, which are valid gauges of the amount and direction of behavior change. The tests might indicate change in the individual's attitudes, his self-perceptions, his insights, his self-controls, and so forth.

On the other hand, it might be feasible to develop standardized rating scales for the staff member who has had most contact with the client to rate the degree and direction of changes in the client, as he sees them. A valid standardized rating scale of this sort should be able to obviate a large part of the prejudicial judgments that enter into the decision to report or not to report violational behavior, to act or not to act. It might even be possible to develop behavioral rating scales, showing directionality over time, by other clients in the same program as the client being rated. (See footnote 1, at the end of this chapter, for a statement on several research efforts that have attempted to measure impact of correctional institutions as perceived by the inmates themselves.)

At any rate, the effort to develop postprogram measures of outcome and directionality must be increased, and the attempt to design and implement workable preventive as well as therapeutic programs must proceed, in spite of failures such as the present project.

CONCLUSIONS

The lessons learned from this study reveal the need for: (1) developing more discriminating evaluations of these who are tending toward and not tending toward delinquency; (2) developing more effective role models; (3) intensifying and extending the presentation of these role models, in order to insure their internalization; (4) training more effective role-model discussion leaders (project teachers); and (5) developing valid instruments to measure behavioral change of the clients at the termination of the program or one or more years after termination.

1. Over a period of years, the principal investigator of this project has tried, through his Ph.D. students, to generate studies of the impact of correctional institutions as the inmate saw it, at the point of his release.

The first study of impact was done by Edward J. Galway under the title of "A Measurement of the Effectiveness of a Reformatory Program," (Ph.D. diss., Ohio State University, 1948). Other theses and dissertations bearing on the same subject and directed by the principal investigator include the following: David Eugene Bright, "A Study of Institutional Impact upon Adult Male Prisoners" (Ph.D. diss., Ohio State University, 1951); M. S. Sabnis, "A Measurement of Impact of Institutional Experience on Inmates of a Training School" (Ph.D. diss., Ohio State University, 1951); Harry Zibners, "The Influence of Short-Term Institutionalization upon Emotionally Disturbed and Delinquent Children" (Master's thesis, Ohio State University, 1954); Mark R. Moran, "Inmate Concept of Self" (Ph.D. diss., Ohio State University, 1954); Jon E. Simpson, "Selected Aspects of Institutionalization as Perceived by the Juvenile Offender" (Ph.D. diss., Ohio State University, 1961).

The latter study was part of a larger project undertaken in 1960 by Professor Walter C. Reckless and his colleague Dr. Thomas G. Eynon. A summary of the research approach and major findings of the first five studies mentioned above was made in an article by the principal investigator entitled "The Impact of Correctional Programmes on Inmates," *British Journal of Delinquency* 6 (September 1955) :138–47. A summary of the Simpson study mentioned above may be found in the following two articles: Jon E. Simpson, Thomas G. Eynon, and Walter C. Reckless, "Institutionalization as Perceived by the Juvenile Offender," *Sociology and Social Research* 48, no. 1 (October 1963) :13–23; Thomas G. Eynon and Jon E. Simpson, "The Boy's Perception of Himself in a State Training School for Delinquents," *Social Service Review* 39, no. 1 (March 1965) :31–37. The reader should also consult the attempt to study the impact of two Borstal institutions (for committed youthful offenders over 16 years of age) and one Approved School (for committed juvenile offenders under 16 years of age) in England during 1958. See Walter C. Reckless and P. P. Shervington "Gauging the Impact of the Institution on the Delinquent Youth," *British Journal of Criminology*, July 1963, pp. 7–23.

Beginning in 1964, the principal investigator and his colleague, Dr. Thomas G. Eynon, undertook to study the impact of a small correctional institution for difficult committed juvenile delinquents (average capacity of 200), called Training Institution Central Ohio, by a behavioral-change rating schedule filled out by the staff member of the institution who knew the released subject the best and by a schedule of perceived impact of the institution as seen through the eyes of the releasee just before his departure. See Thomas G. Eynon, Harry E. Allen and Walter C. Reckless, "Measuring Impact of a Juvenile Correctional Institution by Perceptions of Inmates and Staff," *Journal of Research in Crime and Delinquency* 8, no. 1 (January, 1971) :93–107.

Still more recently, we designed a study of behavior change in boys of 15 years of age, considered by the committing juvenile court and the state's diagnostic center to be very difficult youths. These lads are sent to a well-developed training school for delinquent boys. The project called for before-and-after tests based on self-concept and immaturity-level instruments and for ratings at the point of release from the institution by each individual boy's counselor and dormitory leaders. One year after release from the institution each boy would be rated by his after-care (parole) officer. The records of violational behavior and rearrests would be kept on each lad for a period of one year after release from the training school. The design of this project, therefore, would enable the researcher to make an assessment of before-and-after changes on two different tests, a rating of each boy by his (afternoon-evening) cottage leader, by his institutional counselor, and by his parole officer, and the different measures of behavioral change could then be correlated with the recorded post-release (one year) involvement or lack of involvement in violations and delinquency.

Appendixes

APPENDIX A

CURRICULUM CALENDAR FOR PRESENTATION OF FIVE
SETS OF LESSON PLANS*

CURRICULUM CALENDAR: THE WORLD OF WORK

Date	Lesson Number and Title	Activity
Sept. 27	1. What Is Work?	Film: "You Can Go a Long Way"
28	2. Why Do People Work?	Budget Worksheet
29	3. Skill Level and Job Opportunity	Discussion
30	4. How Do People Work?	Reading— worksheet— discussion
Oct. 1	5. Work in Other Countries	Film: "Life in a Hot Rain Forest"
4	6. Famous Persons and Their Work	Reading— discussion

* Taken from *Youth Development Project: Curriculum Lesson Plans and Supplementary Materials*, by Nason E. Hall, Ellsworth E. Foreman, John F. Hilliard, Wayne C. Murphy, Donald L. Pierce, Judith A. Wesner, and Walter C. Reckless (Columbus: Ohio State University Research Foundation, 1964), pp. 1, 33, 62, 95, and 113. Note that the dates are for the school year 1964–65. Reprinted by permission of the Ohio State University Research Foundation.

5	7. Work as a Part of Survival	Film: "Ant City"
6	8. Problems of Idleness	Stimulus Stories
7	9. Work and the Automobile	Stimulus Story —discussion —map
8	10. Interdependence on the Job	Speaker: Air Force
11	11. QUIZ	
12	12. Society's Interest in the Good Worker	Speaker: Social Security
13	13. Skills and Aptitudes in Work, I	Interest inventory—discussion
14	14. Skills and Aptitudes in Work, II	
15	15. Interests and Skills in Different Jobs	Worksheet—discussion
18	16. Obtainable Work Goals	Speaker: School Counsellor
19	17. Qualities Essential to Success	Tape—discussion
20	18. The Best Worker I know, I	Discussion

21	19. Helping People to Help Themselves	Speaker: Bureau of Employment Services
25	20. What Do Employers Look for in a Worker?	Worksheet
26	21. Getting a Job	Film: "I Want a Job"
27	22. The Best Worker I Know, II	Oral Reports
28	23. EXAMINATION ON UNIT	

CURRICULUM CALENDAR: THE SCHOOL AND YOU

Date	Lesson Number and Title	Activity
Nov. 15	1. The Principal's Job and You	Speaker: Principal
16	2. Education in Our City	Film: "The School Story"
17	3. The Function of School Rules	Discussion
18	4. An Alternative Choice for School	Speaker: Neighborhood Youth Corps
19	5. Preparation for Trip to Central H.S.	Discussion— slides
22	6. Vocational School Trip	Field trip: Central High School
23	7. Organizing Our Time	Speaker: School athlete
24	8. Factors Leading to a Negative Alternative: Drop-out	Stimulus story —discussion
29	9. Overcoming Adversity	Speaker: Alcoholics Anonymous—worksheet
30	10. Review	

Dec.	1	11. Lessons Learned by the Drop-Out	Film: "The Quitters"
	2	12. Trip to School for the Blind	Discussion— Field Trip
	3	13. Alternative Careers and Individual Choice	Worksheet
	6	14. Where Do I Stand?	Discussion— evaluation sheet
	7	15. Play Rehearsal	
	8	16. Sacrificing for Education	Speaker: college student
	9	17. Presentation of Play	
	10	18. EXAMINATION ON UNIT	

CURRICULUM CALENDAR: THE HOUSE WE LIVE IN

Date	Lesson Number and Title	Activity
Jan. 10	1. The Police and Young People	Tape recording: Captain, Police Juvenile Bureau
11	2. Police Selection and Training	Lecture—quiz
12	3. The Policeman as a Person	Speaker: Juvenile Officer
13	4. You and the Law	Reading
14	5. Duties and Rewards of Probation Officer's Job	Speaker: Probation Officer
17	6. Purposes and Operation of the Ohio Youth Commission	Speaker: Ohio Youth Commission—quiz
18	7. Ohio State Highway Patrol	Film: "The Flying Wheel"—Speaker: Highway Patrolman
19	8. The Federal Bureau of Investigation	Film: "The F.B.I."

20	9. Review	
21	10. Your Health Department	Speaker: Ohio Health Dept.
24	11. Welfare Services	Speaker: Social worker— worksheet
25	12. Helping Children Who Can't Help Themselves	Film: "Suffer Little Children"
26	13. Caring for the Mentally Ill	Film: "Out of the Shadows"
27	14. Helping Those with Problems	Speaker: Psychiatrist
31	15. Other State Services	Discussion
Feb. 1	16. Government Services: Forestry	Film: "A Fire Called Jeremiah"
2	17. Government Services: Weather	Film: "The Weather Station"
3	18. Government Services: Meat Inspection	Film: "Meat Inspection Service"
4	19. Respect for the Law	Film: "Why We Respect the Law"

7	20. Case Study	Stimulus story —socio-drama
8	21. Consequences of Moral Decisions	Film: "Right or Wrong"
9	22. EXAMINATION ON UNIT	

CURRICULUM CALENDAR: GETTING ALONG WITH OTHERS

Date	Lesson Number and Title	Activity
Feb. 28	1. Problems in Getting Along with Others, I	Film: "The Trouble-maker"
Mar. 1	2. People We Admire and People We Don't Admire	Discussion
2	3. Problems in Getting Along with Others, II	Film: "The Griper"
3	4. "Yes Man" and "No Man"	Reading—discussion
4	5. What Do Girls Look for in a Young Man?	Girls' Panel Discussion
7	6. Is Personal Appearance Important?	Speaker: Vice Principal
8	7. Practicing Some Common Courtesies	Grooming Inspection—Courtesy Demonstrations

9	8. Telephone Etiquette	TeleTrainer Demonstration
10	9. Good Conduct on the Job: Does It Pay Off?	Stimulus stories
11	10. Getting Along on the Job, I	Film: "The Supervisor as a Leader"
14	11. Getting Along on the Job, II	
15	12. Attitude Is Important	Speaker: Telephone Co. Community Relations Supervisor
16	13. EXAMINATION ON UNIT	

CURRICULUM CALENDAR: THE FAMILY

Date	Lesson Number and Title	Activity
April 4	1. Propagation of the Species	Slides—worksheet
5	2. Reproduction: Plants and Animals	Film: "New Life from Old: Reproduction"
6	3. Reproduction: Humans	Film: "Human Growth"
7	4. Care of the Young: Animals	Field Trip: Columbus Zoo
12	5. Care of the Young: Humans	Film: "Know Your Baby"
13	6. Review	
14	7. Functions Performed by Families in Different Cultures	Film: "Family Living around the World: Family Life"
15	8. Interdependence and Mutual Respect in Families of Different Cultures	Worksheet— discussion

18	9. Family Problems	Stimulus stories—sociodrama
19	10. You and Your Family	Speaker: Catholic Nun
20	11. Review	
21	12. Projective Self-Identification	Discussion—board work
22	13. Family Pathogens: Overcoercion	Worksheet—stimulus story—discussion
25	14. Family Pathogens: Oversubmission	Worksheet—stimulus story—discussion
26	15. Family Pathogens: Punitiveness	Worksheet—stimulus story—discussion
27	16. Family Pathogens: Neglect	Worksheet—stimulus story—discussion
28	17. Pathogen Review	Reading—pathogen worksheet
29	18. Understanding Parents	Film: "Who Should Decide?"

May	2	19. Rights and Re- sponsibilities of Family Members	Reading
	3	20. EXAMINATION ON UNIT	

APPENDIX B

Lesson title: The Best Worker   Lesson number: 18
I know, I

Objectives:
1. To provide the student with further exposure to positive work models.
2. To reinforce previous learning.

Procedures:
1. Discussion leading to development of a guide for an interview with the best worker whom the student knows in his neighborhood.
   a. How can you tell a good worker?
      1. Length of employment at a single firm
      2. Consistency of employment
      3. Takes advantage of training programs
      4. Seldom absent because of sickness, accidents, etc.
      5. Pride in his work
      6. Respected by his fellow workers
2. Discussion: development of interview guide. Elicit questions to be included from pupils. Include items below.

---

* Taken from *Youth Development Project: Curriculum Lesson Plans and Supplementary Materials*, by Nason E. Hall, Ellsworth E. Foreman, John F. Hilliard, Wayne C. Murphy, Donald L. Pierce, Judith A. Wesner, and Walter C. Reckless, (Columbus: Ohio State University Research Foundation, 1964), pp. 26, 47, 88, 98, and 122.

    a. Tell person of your assignment and ask him to tell you about his job—what he actually does.

    b. Ask how long he has worked at the job.

    c. Ask if he has received salary advances over the years or if he has moved up to better jobs. If so, ask him why he thinks he has moved up.

    d. Ask what kind of training he had for his job.

    e. What special benefits other than salary does he get from his job?

    f. How did he get interested in what he is doing?

    g. What does he like about his job?

    h. What does he dislike about his job?

    i. How does he get along with the boss?

    j. Does he think he makes enough money for the work he does?

    k. What are his chances for advancement?

3. Have pupils copy questions selected and assign interviews. Reports are to be given four days later.

Materials: none

Vocabulary:
1. interview
2. benefits
3. assignment
4. neighborhood
5. on-the-job training

Lesson title: Lessons Learned   Lesson number: 11
          by the Drop-Out

Objectives:
  1. To point up the consequences of dropping out of
     school and the advantages of completing high
     school.

Procedures:
  1. "We can often learn from the experiences of
     others." Tell how people differ from animals: ex-
     perience of past generations can be passed on to
     future generations. Animals have to learn every-
     thing anew with each generation.
  2. Introduce film: Today's film deals with the true
     experience of a young man who quit school before
     graduating.
     a. Things to look for
        1. Consequences of dropping out
        2. Reasons for dropping out
     b. Things to think about
        1. Similarities between his school life and
           yours
        2. Do you think he will finish night school?
  3. Show film.
  4. Discussion
     a. Why did Bill leave school?
     b. Were his reasons good?
     c. Why did he go back?
     d. Would you have gone back?
     e. Would he have had it easier if he hadn't quit?
     f. What would have happened if he hadn't gone
        back?

Materials:
1. Film: "The Quitters," 20 min.
2. Movie projector

Vocabulary:
1. limbo
2. Child Labor Law

Lesson title: Case Study   Lesson number: 20

Objectives:
1. To review the several roles played by agencies in helping people with problems.
2. To provide insight into the factors underlying behavior problems.

Procedures:
1. Ask students to name speakers who have come in to talk during the unit. List names on board.
2. Explain sociodrama-stimulus story exercise: after reading the story, several pupils will take the role of speakers and will discuss what they can do to help the boy with his problems.
3. Read story.
4. Panel sociodrama:
   a. Have each role-player address what he can do for mother, boy.
   b. What treatment do they describe?
5. Discussion: Do you think Fred can really be helped?

Materials:
1. Stimulus story: "Fred Johnson"

Vocabulary: none

Lesson title: Problems in Getting   Lesson number: 3
Along with Others, II

Objectives:
1. To show how impressions can lead to lasting undesirable relationships with others.
2. To review process of development of the self-concept.

Procedures:
1. Introduce subject of film and ask students to watch for influences which lead to the boy becoming a griper.
2. Show film.
3. Discussion
   a. What influences made the boy a griper?
   b. How did the other people in the film feel about the Griper?
   c. What is a "show-off"? List characteristics.
   d. What do people think about show-offs?
   e. What is a bragger?
   f. What do people think about braggers?
4. Homework assignment: worksheet. During the year we have had a good chance to see some "poor" habits in our class. List these, and rate them according to the degree to which they bug you. Do the same with "good" habits which make you like some members of the class more.
5. Follow-up: tabulate returns and list on board. Have class vote on two best-liked boys.

Materials:
1. Film: "The Griper," 10 min.
2. Movie projector
3. Worksheet: "Good Habits and Poor Habits"

Vocabulary:
  1. griper
  2. show-off
  3. troublemaker
  4. bully
  5. bragger

Lesson title: Functions Performed   Lesson number:
by Families in   7
Different Cultures

Objectives:
1. To show the purpose of the existence of a family.
2. To show how cultures around the world use the family to perform certain jobs.

Procedures:
1. Introduction: Motivating question—What is the reason a family exists? (Protection, care of young, companionship, training of children to take part in life, control the actions of members, maintain the human race [hopefully].)
2. Show film.
3. Discuss and list six functions of the family. Bring out as examples any functions shown in the film. Tie examples of the functions performed by French Canadian, Eskimo, Malayan, Indian, Greek, and Norwegian families into prior examples of animals and examples in American family life.

Materials:
1. Film: "Family Living around the World: Family Life," 20 min.
2. Movie projector

Vocabulary: none

APPENDIX C

Distribution of Experimental, Control, and Comparison Subjects Who Had Recorded Contacts With Police for Serious, Moderate, and Slight Offenses during Three Time Periods of the Project

Type of Offense	Experimentals				Controls				Comparisons				Total
	Pre	During	Post	Total	Pre	During	Post	Total	Pre	During	Post	Total	
	*(632)	(536)	(536)		(461)	(379)	(379)		(632)	(535)	(535)		
Serious													
Aggravated assault	0	0	4	4	1	0	2	3	0	0	1	1	8
Armed robbery	0	0	1	1	0	0	2	2	0	0	0	0	3
Arson	1	0	0	1	1	0	0	1	0	0	0	0	2
Assault and battery	2	2	16	20	1	2	17	20	1	0	9	10	50
Assault with a deadly weapon	4	0	0	4	0	0	0	0	0	0	0	0	4
Auto theft	2	13	80	95	4	15	47	66	0	0	16	16	177
Breaking and entering	6	7	17	30	4	2	13	19	1	0	5	6	55
Burglary	14	7	24	45	8	5	21	34	4	2	6	12	91
Escape from custody	0	0	0	0	0	0	2	2	0	0	0	0	2
Felonious assault	0	0	0	0	0	0	1	1	0	0	0	0	1
Forgery, fraud	0	0	2	2	0	0	1	1	0	0	0	0	3
Grand larceny	3	3	7	13	1	1	8	10	2	0	1	3	26
Hit and run	0	0	1	1	0	0	1	1	0	0	0	0	2
Housebreaking	10	3	3	16	4	3	9	16	0	2	1	3	35
Influencing a minor	0	0	1	1	0	0	1	1	0	0	1	1	3
Molesting	3	2	4	9	0	1	2	3	0	0	1	1	13
Murder	0	0	1	1	0	0	0	0	0	0	1	1	2
Purse snatching	0	0	3	3	0	0	3	3	0	0	0	0	6
Receiving and concealing stolen property	2	1	7	10	3	1	5	9	0	0	4	4	23
Theft from mail	0	0	0	0	1	0	0	1	0	0	1	1	2
Unarmed robbery	4	1	12	17	1	0	4	5	1	0	0	1	23
Vandalism	1	0	0	1	1	0	0	1	1	0	0	1	3
Sodomy	0	0	0	0	0	0	0	0	0	0	1	1	1
Embezzlement	0	0	1	1	0	0	0	0	0	0	0	0	1
Total	52	39	184	275	30	30	139	199	10	4	48	62	536
Moderate													
Any serious offense attempted investigated	24	36	49	109	20	24	28	72	4	1	13	18	199
Carrying a concealed weapon	1	3	7	11	0	0	6	6	0	0	0	0	17
Glue sniffing	0	0	3	3	0	0	2	2	0	0	0	0	5
Impersonating a police officer or member of armed forces	0	0	1	1	0	0	1	1	0	0	0	0	2
Malicious destruction of property	24	5	13	42	14	4	9	27	5	3	5	13	82
Petit larceny	66	34	53	153	42	12	36	90	7	6	14	27	270

APPENDIX C (continued)

TYPE OF OFFENSE	EXPERIMENTALS				CONTROLS				COMPARISONS				TOTAL
	Pre	During	Post	Total	Pre	During	Post	Total	Pre	During	Post	Total	
Shoplifting	2	1	0	3	1	2	0	3	0	0	1	1	7
Riding in stolen car	0	0	1	1	0	0	0	0	0	0	1	1	2
Starting careless fire	0	0	1	1	1	0	0	1	0	0	0	0	2
Illicit sex with consent	0	0	0	0	0	0	1	1	1	0	0	1	2
Car tampering or stripping	2	0	7	9	1	0	3	4	1	0	4	5	18
Resisting arrest	0	0	3	3	0	0	3	3	0	0	1	1	7
Obscene literature	0	0	1	1	0	0	0	0	0	0	0	0	1
Total	119	79	139	337	79	42	88	209	18	10	40	68	614
Slight													
Curfew violation	5	2	70	77	4	0	57	61	0	0	19	19	157
Discharging firearms in city limits, BB gun	1	1	3	5	0	2	3	5	1	0	4	5	15
Disorderly conduct	3	1	8	12	0	0	9	9	2	0	5	7	28
False fire alarm, false report	3	0	0	3	2	0	2	4	1	0	0	1	8
Fighting	2	0	5	7	2	0	5	7	0	0	1	1	15
Improper language	1	0	2	3	0	0	0	0	0	0	0	0	3
Incorrigibility	11	15	66	92	5	15	42	62	0	1	12	13	167
Intoxication	0	1	9	10	0	0	12	12	0	0	3	3	25
Menacing threats	1	1	0	2	0	0	1	1	0	0	0	0	3
Pointing firearms	0	1	0	1	0	0	0	0	0	0	0	0	1
Possession of fireworks	0	0	4	4	0	0	2	2	0	0	0	0	6
Obstructing justice	0	0	0	0	0	0	1	1	0	0	0	0	1
Suspicious person	0	1	13	14	0	0	5	5	0	1	3	4	23
Swimming in an unguarded area	0	0	0	0	0	0	2	2	1	0	0	1	3
Throwing missiles	1	3	0	4	0	0	1	1	1	0	3	4	9
Trespassing	2	1	10	13	5	2	12	19	2	0	6	8	40
Truancy from home	19	2	52	73	6	3	21	30	1	0	7	8	111
Truancy from school	4	7	0	11	2	5	6	13	2	0	5	7	31
Violating probation	0	2	1	3	0	0	1	1	0	0	0	0	4
Gambling	0	1	3	4	0	0	2	2	0	0	0	0	6
Delinquency	2	0	1	3	3	0	2	5	0	0	2	2	10
Indecent exposure	0	0	0	0	0	0	0	0	0	0	1	1	1
Riding double on a bicycle	1	0	0	1	0	0	0	0	0	0	0	0	1
Failure to appear in court	0	0	1	1	0	0	0	0	0	0	0	0	1
Misrepresentation of minor status	0	0	0	0	0	0	1	1	0	0	0	0	1
Shooting pool	0	0	0	0	0	0	0	0	0	0	1	1	1
Unlawful assembly	0	0	0	0	0	0	0	0	0	0	1	1	1
Total	56	39	248	343	29	27	187	243	11	2	73	86	672
Grand Total	227	157	571	955	138	99	414	651	39	16	161	216	1,822

* Denotes total number of subjects

APPENDIX D

Distribution of Experimental, Control, and Comparison Subjects Who Had Recorded Contacts With Police for Serious, Moderate, and Slight Offenses According to Race.

Type of Offense	Experimentals		Controls		Comparisons		Total	
	White *(322)	Black (310)	White (233)	Black (229)	White (392)	Black (240)	White (947)	Black (779)
Serious								
Aggravated assault	2	2	1	2	0	1	3	5
Armed robbery	0	1	1	1	0	0	1	2
Arson	1	0	1	0	0	0	2	0
Assault and battery	8	12	2	18	4	6	14	36
Assault with a deadly weapon	2	2	0	0	0	0	2	2
Auto theft	34	61	20	46	9	7	63	114
Breaking and entering	10	20	5	14	4	2	19	36
Burglary	18	27	9	25	5	7	32	59
Escape from custody	0	0	1	1	0	0	1	1
Felonious assault	1	1	0	1	0	0	0	1
Forgery	7	6	0	1	2	1	11	2
Grand larceny	7	0	2	8	0	0	2	15
Hit and run	1	0	1	0	1	2	10	0
Housebreaking	4	12	5	11	1	0	1	25
Influencing a minor	0	1	0	1	1	1	3	2
Molesting	2	7	1	2	0	0	2	10
Murder	1	0	0	0	1	0	0	0
Purse snatching	0	3	0	3	0	2	7	6
Receiving and concealing stolen property	4	6	1	8	2	2	1	16
Theft from the mail	0	0	1	0	0	1	1	1
Unarmed robbery	0	17	1	4	1	0	2	21
Vandalism, over $50 damage	1	0	0	1	1	0	2	1

APPENDIX D (continued)

Type of Offense	Experimentals		Controls		Comparisons		Total	
	White	Black	White	Black	White	Black	White	Black
Sodomy	1	0	0	0	0	0	1	0
Embezzlement	1	0	0	0	0	0	1	0
Total	97	178	52	147	31	31	180	356
Moderate								
Any serious offense attempted or investigated	30	79	22	50	11	7	63	136
Carrying a concealed weapon	0	10	2	4	0	0	2	14
Glue sniffing	1	2	0	2	0	0	1	4
Impersonating a police officer or a member of the armed forces	0	1	1	0	0	0	1	1
Malicious destruction of property	21	21	11	16	8	5	40	42
Petit larceny	53	100	22	68	15	12	90	180
Shoplifting	2	1	2	1	1	0	5	2
Riding in a stolen car	0	1	0	0	0	1	0	2
Illicit sex with consent	1	1	0	0	1	1	2	1
Starting a careless fire	1	0	0	1	0	0	1	1
Car tampering or stripping	1	8	1	3	2	3	4	14
Resisting arrest	0	1	0	0	0	0	0	1
Obscene literature	0	1	0	0	0	0	0	1
Total	112	225	63	146	38	30	213	401
Slight								
Curfew violation	44	33	20	41	14	5	78	79
Discharging firearms in city limits, BB gun	2	3	3	2	4	1	9	6
Disorderly conduct	6	6	3	6	4	3	13	15
False fire alarm, false report	2	1	3	1	0	1	5	3
Fighting	3	4	1	6	0	1	4	11

APPENDIX D (continued)

TYPE OF OFFENSE	EXPERIMENTALS White	EXPERIMENTALS Black	CONTROLS White	CONTROLS Black	COMPARISONS White	COMPARISONS Black	TOTAL White	TOTAL Black
Improper language	0	3	0	0	0	0	0	3
Incorrigibility	48	44	25	37	8	5	81	86
Intoxication	6	5	6	3	4	1	16	9
Menacing threats	0	2	1	0	0	0	1	2
Pointing firearms	0	0	1	0	0	0	1	0
Possession of fireworks	2	4	0	0	0	0	2	4
Obstructing justice	0	0	0	1	0	0	0	1
Suspicious person	7	7	3	2	2	2	12	11
Swimming in an unguarded area	3	0	0	0	0	0	3	0
Throwing missiles	0	4	1	2	1	1	2	7
Tresspassing	6	7	10	9	7	1	23	17
Truancy from home	46	16	16	20	10	3	72	39
Truancy from school	10	5	4	6	5	1	19	12
Violating probation	1	1	0	1	0	1	1	3
Gambling	0	3	0	3	0	0	0	6
Delinquency	2	3	1	4	0	0	3	7
Indecent exposure	0	0	0	0	1	0	1	0
Riding double on a bicycle	0	1	0	0	0	0	0	1
Failure to appear in court	1	0	0	0	0	0	1	0
Misrepresentation of minor status	1	0	1	0	0	0	1	0
Shooting pool	0	0	1	0	0	0	1	0
Unlawful assembly	0	1	0	0	0	0	0	1
Total	190	153	99	144	60	26	349	323
Grand Total	399	556	214	437	129	87	742	1,080

* Denotes total number of subjects.

APPENDIX E

1963–1964 SCHEDULE

A. Name _____

B. What is the name of the school you attended last spring? _____

C. What is the name of the school you will attend in September? _____

D. What grade will you be in? _____

E. When were you born? Month _____ day ____ year _____

F. Write in the names of your two best friends at the school you attended last year.

_____

_____

HOW I FEEL ABOUT THINGS

Read each sentence and circle "T" for *True* and "F" for *False*.

T F 1. A person is better off if he doesn't trust anyone.

T F 2. I used to give the teachers lots of trouble.

T F 3. It is very important to me to have enough friends.

T F 4. I seem to do things that I regret more often than other people do.

T F 5. I would rather go without something than ask for a favor.

T F 6. I have had more than my share of things to worry about.

T F 7. I go out of my way to meet trouble rather than try to escape it.

T F 8. When I meet a stranger, I often think that he is better than I am.

T F 9. I was sometimes sent to the principal for cutting up.

T F 10. I keep out of trouble at all costs.

T F 11. Most of the time I feel happy.

T F 12. I played hookey quite often.

T F 13. People often talk about me behind my back.

T F 14. I don't think I'm quite as happy as others seem to be.

T F 15. I never cared much for school.

THE WAY IT LOOKS TO ME

Read each sentence. Then circle "Y" for *Yes* and "N" for *No*.

Y N 1. If you found that a friend was leading you into trouble, would you continue to run around with him or her?

Y N 2. Do you plan to finish high school?

Y N 3. Do you think you'll stay out of trouble in the future?

Y N 4. Are grown-ups usually against you?

Y N 5. If you could get permission to work at 14, would you quit school?

Y N 6. Are you a big shot with your pals?

Y N 7. Do you think if you were to get into trouble with the law, it would be bad for you in the future?

IS THIS LIKE YOU OR NOT LIKE YOU?

Read each statement and then put an "X" in front of the answer that you think is most like you.

1. I can see as good (with glasses, if I wear them) and I can hear as good as most other people can.

_____ Like me   _____ Not like me

2. I often feel tired and "all in" even when I haven't been working hard.

_____ Like me   _____ Not like me

3. If I can't do something the first time, I don't mind spending a lot of time trying to figure out other ways to do it.

_____ Like me   _____ Not like me

4. I thought that just about every book in school was too tough for students to understand by themselves.

_____ Like me   _____ Not like me

5. I would find things a lot easier if I didn't keep making the same mistake over and over again.

_____ Like me   _____ Not like me

6. Even when somebody doesn't agree with me, I can usually understand his reasons for not agreeing with me.

_____ Like me   _____ Not like me

7. I trust the judgment of my friends more often than I do my own judgment.

_____ Like me   _____ Not like me

8. I often make up my mind after it is too late.

_____ Like me   _____ Not like me

9. Too many things just don't turn out the way I expect them to.

_____ Like me   _____ Not like me

10. I often get into hot water because I speak or act without thinking.

_____ Like me   _____ Not like me

11. I often find myself with a lot of time on my hands with nothing to do.

_____ Like me   _____ Not like me

WHO AM I?

In the blanks below write as many answers as you can to the question "Who am I?" Don't take more than five minutes.

1. _____

2. _____

3. _____

4. _____

5. _____

6. _____

7. _____

8. _____

9. _____

10. _____

WHO ARE THE MOST IMPORTANT ADULTS IN MY LIFE?

Think about the adults who mean the most to you and are the most important to you. Do not write their names only who they are. The most important one of all comes first. The next important one comes next, and so forth. It is up to you to put down as many adults as you think are important. Remember, no kids—just adults.

1. (The most important adult to you) _____
2. (The next most important adult to you) _____
3. (The next important) _____
4. (The next important) _____
5. (The next important) _____
6. (The next important) _____
7. (The next important) _____
8. (The next important) _____
9. (The next important) _____
10. (The next important) _____

APPENDIX F

1964–66 Schedule

PLEASE PRINT   Date _____

A. Name _____
        Last   First   Middle

B. Address _____
        Number   Street

C. What is the name of your school? _____

D. When were you born? Month _____ Day ____
    Year _____

E. Father's name _____
        Last   First   Middle

F. Mother's name _____
        Last   First   Middle

G. With whom do you live?

    ____ Mother and father

    ____ Mother only

    ____ Father only

    ____ Stepmother and stepfather

    ____ Mother and stepfather

    ____ Father and stepmother

    ____ Other (Explain) _____
        (uncle, aunt, grandmother, grandfather, no relationship)

H. What kind of work does your father or stepfather do? _____

I. Does your mother or stepmother earn money for the family? _____

If yes, what kind of work does she do? _____

J. If you live with someone else ("Other" checked in question G), what kind of work does he or she do?

_____

This is not a test. There are no right and wrong answers. The reason for asking these questions is to find out how boys like you *really* feel about things. We want your honest answers to these questions.

Read each statement very carefully and circle the single answer that best tells how you feel about the statement. Circle STRONGLY AGREE, AGREE, UNDECIDED, DISAGREE, or STRONGLY DISAGREE, whichever you feel is the closest to your feelings about the statement.

1. I am not smart enough to go to college.

STRONGLY AGREE   AGREE   UNDECIDED   DISAGREE
STRONGLY DISAGREE

2. Most teachers never really give a kid a break.

STRONGLY AGREE   AGREE   UNDECIDED   DISAGREE
STRONGLY DISAGREE

3. The better our education, the better use we can make of our time.

STRONGLY AGREE   AGREE   UNDECIDED   DISAGREE
STRONGLY DISAGREE

4. Most teachers don't like me.

STRONGLY AGREE   AGREE   UNDECIDED   DISAGREE
STRONGLY DISAGREE

5. Most teachers like to teach school.

STRONGLY AGREE   AGREE   UNDECIDED   DISAGREE
STRONGLY DISAGREE

6. I am proud of my school.

STRONGLY AGREE   AGREE   UNDECIDED   DISAGREE
STRONGLY DISAGREE

7. Most kids don't have as much trouble learning as I do.

STRONGLY AGREE   AGREE   UNDECIDED   DISAGREE STRONGLY DISAGREE

8. Most teachers try to treat all kids fairly.

STRONGLY AGREE   AGREE   UNDECIDED   DISAGREE STRONGLY DISAGREE

9. Grown-ups don't really think school does any good.

STRONGLY AGREE   AGREE   UNDECIDED   DISAGREE STRONGLY DISAGREE

10. I like most of my teachers.

STRONGLY AGREE   AGREE   UNDECIDED   DISAGREE STRONGLY DISAGREE

11. Most teachers really know the subjects they teach.

STRONGLY AGREE   AGREE   UNDECIDED   DISAGREE STRONGLY DISAGREE

12. Going to school keeps a lot of kids out of trouble.

STRONGLY AGREE   AGREE   UNDECIDED   DISAGREE STRONGLY DISAGREE

13. I am smarter than most of the other kids in the 7th grade.

STRONGLY AGREE   AGREE   UNDECIDED   DISAGREE STRONGLY DISAGREE

14. Most teachers are often unfair.

STRONGLY AGREE   AGREE   UNDECIDED   DISAGREE STRONGLY DISAGREE

15. Education helps you to understand the world around you.

STRONGLY AGREE   AGREE   UNDECIDED   DISAGREE STRONGLY DISAGREE

16. It is usually the teacher's fault when I get into trouble at school.

STRONGLY AGREE   AGREE   UNDECIDED   DISAGREE
STRONGLY DISAGREE

17. Most teachers do a very good job of helping kids.

STRONGLY AGREE   AGREE   UNDECIDED   DISAGREE
STRONGLY DISAGREE

18. I enjoy going to school.

STRONGLY AGREE   AGREE   UNDECIDED   DISAGREE
STRONGLY DISAGREE

19. I am smart enough to become a doctor or lawyer.

STRONGLY AGREE   AGREE   UNDECIDED   DISAGREE
STRONGLY DISAGREE

20. Most teachers understand kids.

STRONGLY AGREE   AGREE   UNDECIDED   DISAGREE
STRONGLY DISAGREE

21. School makes you feel like you're important.

STRONGLY AGREE   AGREE   UNDECIDED   DISAGREE
STRONGLY DISAGREE

22. Teachers often fuss at me for no reason.

STRONGLY AGREE   AGREE   UNDECIDED   DISAGREE
STRONGLY DISAGREE

23. Most teachers have trouble making school work interesting.

STRONGLY AGREE   AGREE   UNDECIDED   DISAGREE
STRONGLY DISAGREE

24. Homework is a waste of time.

STRONGLY AGREE   AGREE   UNDECIDED   DISAGREE
STRONGLY DISAGREE

25. I am not really smart enough to do well in school.

STRONGLY AGREE   AGREE   UNDECIDED   DISAGREE
STRONGLY DISAGREE

26. Teachers should not correct kids in front of other kids.

STRONGLY AGREE   AGREE   UNDECIDED   DISAGREE
STRONGLY DISAGREE

27. Making more money is the main reason for getting an education.

STRONGLY AGREE   AGREE   UNDECIDED   DISAGREE
STRONGLY DISAGREE

28. My teachers think I am headed for serious trouble.

STRONGLY AGREE   AGREE   UNDECIDED   DISAGREE
STRONGLY DISAGREE

29. Most teachers don't like to flunk students.

STRONGLY AGREE   AGREE   UNDECIDED   DISAGREE
STRONGLY DISAGREE

30. I feel very bad when I don't pass a test.

STRONGLY AGREE   AGREE   UNDECIDED   DISAGREE
STRONGLY DISAGREE

31. School makes me feel dumber than most kids.

STRONGLY AGREE   AGREE   UNDECIDED   DISAGREE
STRONGLY DISAGREE

32. Most teachers are too strict with their kids.

STRONGLY AGREE   AGREE   UNDECIDED   DISAGREE
STRONGLY DISAGREE

33. The only advantage in going to school is to get a better job.

STRONGLY AGREE   AGREE   UNDECIDED   DISAGREE
STRONGLY DISAGREE

34. I would like to tell most of my teachers what I really think of them.

STRONGLY AGREE   AGREE   UNDECIDED   DISAGREE
STRONGLY DISAGREE

35. Most teachers try to help kids with their school work as much as possible.

STRONGLY AGREE   AGREE   UNDECIDED   DISAGREE
STRONGLY DISAGREE

36. My parents are interested in my school.

STRONGLY AGREE   AGREE   UNDECIDED   DISAGREE
STRONGLY DISAGREE

37. No matter how hard I try, I will never learn some subjects.

STRONGLY AGREE   AGREE   UNDECIDED   DISAGREE
STRONGLY DISAGREE

38. Most teachers like kids.

STRONGLY AGREE   AGREE   UNDECIDED   DISAGREE
STRONGLY DISAGREE

39. Teachers often take advantage of me.

STRONGLY AGREE   AGREE   UNDECIDED   DISAGREE
STRONGLY DISAGREE

40. Most teachers are very good at teaching.

STRONGLY AGREE   AGREE   UNDECIDED   DISAGREE
STRONGLY DISAGREE

41. I don't think the school rules are fair.

STRONGLY AGREE   AGREE   UNDECIDED   DISAGREE
STRONGLY DISAGREE

42. Most school work is too hard for me.

STRONGLY AGREE   AGREE   UNDECIDED   DISAGREE
STRONGLY DISAGREE

43. Most teachers enjoy paddling kids.

STRONGLY AGREE   AGREE   UNDECIDED   DISAGREE
STRONGLY DISAGREE

44. I give my teachers lots of trouble.

STRONGLY AGREE   AGREE   UNDECIDED   DISAGREE
STRONGLY DISAGREE

45. Kids should be permitted to quit school at any age.

STRONGLY AGREE   AGREE   UNDECIDED   DISAGREE
STRONGLY DISAGREE

46. Most teachers have some kids who are their pets.

STRONGLY AGREE   AGREE   UNDECIDED   DISAGREE
STRONGLY DISAGREE

47. School is a place where a kid must obey a lot of unnecessary rules.

STRONGLY AGREE   AGREE   UNDECIDED   DISAGREE
STRONGLY DISAGREE

48. School is a place where a kid can lose his temper easily.

STRONGLY AGREE   AGREE   UNDECIDED   DISAGREE
STRONGLY DISAGREE

49. Most policemen don't care what happens to kids.

STRONGLY AGREE   AGREE   UNDECIDED   DISAGREE
STRONGLY DISAGREE

50. Policemen have no right to tell kids what to do.

STRONGLY AGREE   AGREE   UNDECIDED   DISAGREE
STRONGLY DISAGREE

51. It doesn't take very much ability to be a policeman.

STRONGLY AGREE   AGREE   UNDECIDED   DISAGREE
STRONGLY DISAGREE

52. Most probation officers don't care what happens to the kids with whom they work.

STRONGLY AGREE   AGREE   UNDECIDED   DISAGREE
STRONGLY DISAGREE

53. Kids would be better off if there were fewer probation officers.

STRONGLY AGREE   AGREE   UNDECIDED   DISAGREE
STRONGLY DISAGREE

54. If a Juvenile Court sends a kid to training school, it is because it is the best thing for him in the long run.

STRONGLY AGREE   AGREE   UNDECIDED   DISAGREE
STRONGLY DISAGREE

55. We would be better off if we didn't have any Juvenile Courts.

STRONGLY AGREE   AGREE   UNDECIDED   DISAGREE
STRONGLY DISAGREE

56. Laws protect the rights of kids.

STRONGLY AGREE   AGREE   UNDECIDED   DISAGREE
STRONGLY DISAGREE

57. There are too many laws.

STRONGLY AGREE   AGREE   UNDECIDED   DISAGREE
STRONGLY DISAGREE

58. Most policemen like to help kids.

STRONGLY AGREE   AGREE   UNDECIDED   DISAGREE
STRONGLY DISAGREE

59. Life would be better if there were not as many policemen.

STRONGLY AGREE   AGREE   UNDECIDED   DISAGREE
STRONGLY DISAGREE

60. Most policemen are poorly trained for their job.

STRONGLY AGREE   AGREE   UNDECIDED   DISAGREE
STRONGLY DISAGREE

61. Most probation officers enjoy ordering kids around.

STRONGLY AGREE   AGREE   UNDECIDED   DISAGREE
STRONGLY DISAGREE

62. Probation officers have no right to tell a kid what to do.

STRONGLY AGREE   AGREE   UNDECIDED   DISAGREE
STRONGLY DISAGREE

63. Juvenile Courts are only interested in convicting a lot of kids.

STRONGLY AGREE AGREE UNDECIDED DISAGREE
STRONGLY DISAGREE

64. Juvenile Courts are necessary in our way of life.

STRONGLY AGREE AGREE UNDECIDED DISAGREE
STRONGLY DISAGREE

65. The law always works against a kid, never for him.

STRONGLY AGREE AGREE UNDECIDED DISAGREE
STRONGLY DISAGREE

66. It is all right to break the law if you don't get caught.

STRONGLY AGREE AGREE UNDECIDED DISAGREE
STRONGLY DISAGREE

67. Most policemen like to pick on kids.

STRONGLY AGREE AGREE UNDECIDED DISAGREE
STRONGLY DISAGREE

68. Policemen have too much authority.

STRONGLY AGREE AGREE UNDECIDED DISAGREE
STRONGLY DISAGREE

69. Most policemen are pretty nice guys.

STRONGLY AGREE AGREE UNDECIDED DISAGREE
STRONGLY DISAGREE

70. Most probation officers want to help kids.

STRONGLY AGREE AGREE UNDECIDED DISAGREE
STRONGLY DISAGREE

71. Probation is a waste of time.

STRONGLY AGREE AGREE UNDECIDED DISAGREE
STRONGLY DISAGREE

72. Juvenile Courts are interested in doing what is best for a kid.

STRONGLY AGREE AGREE UNDECIDED DISAGREE
STRONGLY DISAGREE

73. Juvenile Courts have too much authority.

STRONGLY AGREE   AGREE   UNDECIDED   DISAGREE
STRONGLY DISAGREE

74. Laws are only made to give kids a hard time.

STRONGLY AGREE   AGREE   UNDECIDED   DISAGREE
STRONGLY DISAGREE

75. Laws are made to be broken.

STRONGLY AGREE   AGREE   UNDECIDED   DISAGREE
STRONGLY DISAGREE

76. Most policemen don't understand a kid's problems.

STRONGLY AGREE   AGREE   UNDECIDED   DISAGREE
STRONGLY DISAGREE

77. Without policemen it would not be safe to walk the streets.

STRONGLY AGREE   AGREE   UNDECIDED   DISAGREE
STRONGLY DISAGREE

78. Most policemen like to act tough.

STRONGLY AGREE   AGREE   UNDECIDED   DISAGREE
STRONGLY DISAGREE

79. Most probation officers try to help kids stay out of trouble.

STRONGLY AGREE   AGREE   UNDECIDED   DISAGREE
STRONGLY DISAGREE

80. We need more probation officers.

STRONGLY AGREE   AGREE   UNDECIDED   DISAGREE
STRONGLY DISAGREE

81. Juvenile Courts place kids on probation in order to help them.

STRONGLY AGREE   AGREE   UNDECIDED   DISAGREE
STRONGLY DISAGREE

82. I would like to be a Juvenile Court judge.

STRONGLY AGREE   AGREE   UNDECIDED   DISAGREE
STRONGLY DISAGREE

83. Almost everything that is fun for a kid to do is against the law.

STRONGLY AGREE   AGREE   UNDECIDED   DISAGREE
STRONGLY DISAGREE

84. All laws should be obeyed.

STRONGLY AGREE   AGREE   UNDECIDED   DISAGREE
STRONGLY DISAGREE

85. Most policemen don't give kids a chance to explain.

STRONGLY AGREE   AGREE   UNDECIDED   DISAGREE
STRONGLY DISAGREE

86. We need more policemen.

STRONGLY AGREE   AGREE   UNDECIDED   DISAGREE
STRONGLY DISAGREE

87. Most policemen are honest.

STRONGLY AGREE   AGREE   UNDECIDED   DISAGREE
STRONGLY DISAGREE

88. Most probation officers treat kids rough.

STRONGLY AGREE   AGREE   UNDECIDED   DISAGREE
STRONGLY DISAGREE

89. I would like to be a probation officer.

STRONGLY AGREE   AGREE   UNDECIDED   DISAGREE
STRONGLY DISAGREE

90. Juvenile Courts don't understand a kid's problems.

STRONGLY AGREE   AGREE   UNDECIDED   DISAGREE
STRONGLY DISAGREE

91. "Who you know" is what counts in the Juvenile Court.

STRONGLY AGREE   AGREE   UNDECIDED   DISAGREE
STRONGLY DISAGREE

92. Laws are harder on kids than on adults.

STRONGLY AGREE   AGREE   UNDECIDED   DISAGREE
STRONGLY DISAGREE

93. Laws should be enforced more strictly.

STRONGLY AGREE   AGREE   UNDECIDED   DISAGREE
STRONGLY DISAGREE

94. Once a kid gets into trouble, police keep on hounding him.

STRONGLY AGREE   AGREE   UNDECIDED   DISAGREE
STRONGLY DISAGREE

95. I would like to be a policeman.

STRONGLY AGREE   AGREE   UNDECIDED   DISAGREE
STRONGLY DISAGREE

96. Most probation officers don't really understand a kid's problems.

STRONGLY AGREE   AGREE   UNDECIDED   DISAGREE
STRONGLY DISAGREE

97. A kid is not placed on probation for punishment.

STRONGLY AGREE   AGREE   UNDECIDED   DISAGREE
STRONGLY DISAGREE

98. Poor kids don't have a chance in Juvenile Court.

STRONGLY AGREE   AGREE   UNDECIDED   DISAGREE
STRONGLY DISAGREE

99. Juvenile Courts have no right to tell kids what to do.

STRONGLY AGREE   AGREE   UNDECIDED   DISAGREE
STRONGLY DISAGREE

100. We would be better off if there were not so many laws.

STRONGLY AGREE   AGREE   UNDECIDED   DISAGREE
STRONGLY DISAGREE

101. Most policemen go out of their way to keep a kid out of trouble.

STRONGLY AGREE   AGREE   UNDECIDED   DISAGREE
STRONGLY DISAGREE

102. Policemen should be paid more for their work.

STRONGLY AGREE   AGREE   UNDECIDED   DISAGREE
STRONGLY DISAGREE

103. Most probation officers don't give a kid a chance to explain.

STRONGLY AGREE   AGREE   UNDECIDED   DISAGREE
STRONGLY DISAGREE

104. Probation officers have too much authority.

STRONGLY AGREE   AGREE   UNDECIDED   DISAGREE
STRONGLY DISAGREE

105. A kid can't get justice in Juvenile Court.

STRONGLY AGREE   AGREE   UNDECIDED   DISAGREE
STRONGLY DISAGREE

106. Juvenile Courts have no right to take kids away from their homes.

STRONGLY AGREE   AGREE   UNDECIDED   DISAGREE
STRONGLY DISAGREE

107. We should obey the law even though we criticize it at times.

STRONGLY AGREE   AGREE   UNDECIDED   DISAGREE
STRONGLY DISAGREE

108. Policemen are easier on rich kids than on poor kids.

STRONGLY AGREE   AGREE   UNDECIDED   DISAGREE
STRONGLY DISAGREE

109. Juvenile Courts never give a kid a break.

STRONGLY AGREE   AGREE   UNDECIDED   DISAGREE
STRONGLY DISAGREE

110. Everyone breaks the law from time to time.

STRONGLY AGREE   AGREE   UNDECIDED   DISAGREE
STRONGLY DISAGREE

111. Most policemen are careful not to arrest innocent kids.

STRONGLY AGREE   AGREE   UNDECIDED   DISAGREE
STRONGLY DISAGREE

How do you look at these things? Remember, the right answer for you is the way you look at things.

1. A teen-age boy should always tiptoe around the house.

STRONGLY AGREE   AGREE   UNDECIDED   DISAGREE
STRONGLY DISAGREE

2. Girls should not have hot rods.

STRONGLY AGREE   AGREE   UNDECIDED   DISAGREE
STRONGLY DISAGREE

3. People should only keep promises when it is to their benefit.

STRONGLY AGREE   AGREE   UNDECIDED   DISAGREE
STRONGLY DISAGREE

4. Doing a good job makes a person feel good.

STRONGLY AGREE   AGREE   UNDECIDED   DISAGREE
STRONGLY DISAGREE

5. Good manners are for sissies.

STRONGLY AGREE   AGREE   UNDECIDED   DISAGREE
STRONGLY DISAGREE

6. Finders, keepers: if a person loses something, it belongs to the guy who finds it.

STRONGLY AGREE   AGREE   UNDECIDED   DISAGREE
STRONGLY DISAGREE

7. It's mostly luck if one succeeds or fails.

STRONGLY AGREE   AGREE   UNDECIDED   DISAGREE
STRONGLY DISAGREE

8. It's more fun going to a playground than hanging around the street corner.

STRONGLY AGREE   AGREE   UNDECIDED   DISAGREE
STRONGLY DISAGREE

9. Don't let anybody your size get by with anything.

STRONGLY AGREE   AGREE   UNDECIDED   DISAGREE
STRONGLY DISAGREE

10. It's worth practicing to get good at something.

STRONGLY AGREE   AGREE   UNDECIDED   DISAGREE
STRONGLY DISAGREE

11. Money is meant to be spent.

STRONGLY AGREE   AGREE   UNDECIDED   DISAGREE
STRONGLY DISAGREE

12. Loafing is a waste of time.

STRONGLY AGREE   AGREE   UNDECIDED   DISAGREE
STRONGLY DISAGREE

APPENDIX G

SCHOOL AND LAW GUTTMAN SCALES

ORDER AND CUTTING POINTS WITH DIRECTION OF SCORING FOR ITEMS IN EACH GUTTMAN SCALE*

Item No. on
Questionaire   CAPACITY TO LEARN SCALE (CR = .90)

7   Most kids don't have as much trouble learning as I do.
(− SA, A, U, D/ SD +)

1   I am not smart enough to go to college.
(− SA, A, U, D/ SD +)

19   I am smart enough to become a doctor or lawyer.
(+ SA, A/ U, D, SD −)

13   I am smarter than most of the other kids in the 7th grade.
(+ SA, A, U/ D, SD −)

42   Most school work is too hard for me.
(− SA, A/ U, D, SD +)

---

* Items are ordered in terms of their position in the scale. Plus (+) equals the direction of favorable score, and minus (−) equals the direction of unfavorable score. SA = Strongly Agree, A = Agree, U = Undecided, D = Disagree, and SD = Strongly Disagree. The symbol / indicates the cutting point for favorable and unfavorable directions. CR = Coefficient of Reproducibility on first administration.

25   I am not really smart enough to do
            well in school.
            (− SA, A/ U, D, SD +)

VALUE OF EDUCATION SCALE (CR = .90)

33   The only advantage in going to school
            is to get a better job.
            (− SA, A, U, D/ SD +)

27   Making more money is the main rea-
            son for getting an education.
            (− SA, A, U/ D, SD +)

15   Education helps you to understand
            the world around you.
            (+ SA/ A, U, D, SD −)

9   Grown-ups don't really think school
            does any good.
            (− SA/ A, U, D/ SD +)

21   School makes you feel like you're im-
            portant.
            (+ SA, A, U/ D, SD −)

LEGITIMACY OF SCHOOL SCALE (CR = .91)

47   School is a place where a kid must
            obey a lot of unnecessary rules.
            (− SA, A, U/ D, SD +)

30   I feel very bad when I don't pass a
            test.
            (+ SA/ A, U, D, SD −)

12   Going to school keeps a lot of kids out
            of trouble.
            (+ SA/ A, U, D, SD −)

45	Kids should be permitted to quit school at any age. (− SA, A/ U, D, SD +)
18	I enjoy going to school. (+ SA, A, U, D/ SD −)
6	I am proud of my school. (+ SA, A, U/ D, SD −)
24	Homework is a waste of time. (− SA/ A, U, D, SD +)

TEACHERS—ACADEMIC SCALE (CR = .92)

23	Most teachers have trouble making school work interesting. (− SA, A, U, D/ SD +)
40	Most teachers are very good at teaching. (+ SA/ A, U, D, SD −)
35	Most teachers try to help kids with their school work as much as possible. (+ SA/ A, U, D, SD −)
11	Most teachers really know the subjects they teach. (+ SA/ A, U, D, SD −)
5	Most teachers like to teach school. (+ SA, A, U/ D, SD −)

TEACHERS—GENERAL SCALE (CR = .90)

32	Most teachers are too strict with their kids. (− SA, A, U, D/ SD +)
14	Most teachers are often unfair. (− SA, A, U, D/ SD +)

20   Most teachers understand kids.
            (+ SA/ A, U, D, SD −)
8   Most teachers try to treat all kids
            fairly.
            (+ SA/ A, U, D, SD −)
2   Most teachers never really give a kid
            a break.
            (− SA, A/ U, D, SD +)
26   Teachers should not correct kids in
            front of other kids.
            (− SA/ A, U, D, SD +)
43   Most teachers enjoy paddling kids.
            (− SA/ A, U, D, SD +)
38   Most teachers like kids.
            (+ SA, A, U/ D, SD −)

TEACHERS—PERSONAL SCALE (CR = .90)

34   I would like to tell most of my teach-
            ers what I really think of them.
            (− SA, A, U/ D, SD +)
16   It is usually the teacher's fault when
            I get into trouble at school.
            (− SA, A, U, D/ SD +)
22   Teachers often fuss at me for no rea-
            son.
            (− SA, A/ U, D, SD +)
39   Teachers often take advantage of me.
            (− SA, A/ U, D, SD +)
28   My teachers think I am headed for
            serious trouble.
            (− SA, A/ U, D, SD +)

4	Most teachers don't like me.
	(− SA, A/ U, D, SD +)
10	I like most of my teachers.
	(+ SA, A/ U, D, SD −)

POLICEMEN—RELATIONSHIP WITH KIDS (CR = .91)

111	Most policemen are careful not to arrest innocent kids.
	(+ SA/ A, U, D, SD −)
67	Most policemen like to pick on kids.
	(− SA, A, U, D/ SD +)
58	Most policemen like to help kids.
	(+ SA/ A, U, D, SD −)
94	Once a kid gets into trouble, police keep on hounding him.
	(− SA, A, U/ D, SD +)
76	Most policemen don't understand a kid's problems.
	(− SA, A/ U, D, SD +)
101	Most policemen go out of their way to keep a kid out of trouble.
	(+ SA, A/ U, D, SD −)
85	Most policemen don't give kids a chance to explain.
	(− SA/ A, U, D, SD +)
108	Policemen are easier on rich kids than on poor kids.
	(− SA/ A, U, D, SD +)
49	Most policemen don't care what happens to kids.
	(− SA, A/ U, D, SD +)

POLICEMEN—LEGITIMACY (CR = .93)

95   I would like to be a policeman.
(+ SA/ A, U, D, SD −)

68   Policemen have too much authority.
(− SA, A, U, D/ SD +)

102   Policemen should be paid more for their work.
(+ SA/ A, U, D, SD −)

77   Without policemen it would not be safe to walk the streets.
(+ SA/ A, U, D, SD −)

86   We need more policemen.
(+ SA, A, U/ D, SD −)

50   Policemen have no right to tell kids what to do.
(− SA, A/ U, D, SD +)

59   Life would be better if there were not as many policemen.
(− SA, A, U/ D, SD +)

POLICEMEN—CHARACTERISTICS (CR = .93)

78   Most policemen like to act tough.
(− SA, A, U, D/ SD +)

87   Most policemen are honest.
(+ SA/ A, U, D, SD −)

69   Most policemen are pretty nice guys.
(+ SA/ A, U, D, SD −)

60   Most policemen are poorly trained for their job.
(− SA, A, U, D/ SD +)

| 51 | It doesn't take very much ability to be a policeman.
($-$ SA, A/ U, D, SD $+$) |

PROBATION OFFICERS—RELATIONSHIP WITH KIDS
(CR $= .95$)

96	Most probation officers don't really understand a kid's problems. ($-$ SA, A, U, D/ SD $+$)
88	Most probation officers treat kids rough. ($-$ SA, A, U, D/ SD $+$)
103	Most probation officers don't give a kid a chance to explain. ($-$ SA, A, U, D/ SD $+$)
79	Most probation officers try to help kids stay out of trouble. ($+$ SA/ A, U, D, SD $-$)
70	Most probation officers want to help kids. ($+$ SA/ A, U, D, SD $-$)
61	Most probation officers enjoy ordering kids around. ($-$ SA, A/ U, D, SD $+$)
52	Most probation officers don't care what happens to the kids with whom they work. ($-$ SA, A/ U, D, SD $+$)

PROBATION OFFICERS—LEGITIMACY (CR $= .87$)

| 104 | Probation officers have too much authority.
($-$ SA, A, U, D/ SD $+$) |

80	We need more probation officers. ($+$ SA/ A, U, D, SD $-$)
89	I would like to be a probation officer. ($+$ SA, A, U/ D, SD $-$)
62	Probation officers have no right to tell a kid what to do. ($-$ SA, A, U, D/ SD $+$)
97	A kid is not placed on probation for punishment. ($+$ SA, A, U/ D, SD $-$)
71	Probation is a waste of time. ($-$ SA, A/ U, D, SD $+$)
53	Kids would be better off if there were fewer probation officers. ($-$ SA, A/ U, D, SD $+$)

COURTS—RELATIONSHIP WITH KIDS (CR $= .93$)

90	Juvenile Courts don't understand a kid's problems. ($-$ SA, A, U, D/ SD $+$)
105	A kid can't get justice in Juvenile Court. ($-$ SA, A, U, D/ SD $+$)
98	Poor kids don't have a chance in Juvenile Court. ($-$ SA, A, U, D/ SD $+$)
63	Juvenile Courts are only interested in convicting a lot of kids. ($-$ SA, A, U, D/ SD $+$)
72	Juvenile Courts are interested in doing what is best for a kid. ($+$ SA/ A, U, D, SD $-$)

54   If a Juvenile Court sends a kid to training school, it is because it is the best thing for him in the long run.
(+ SA, A, U/ D, SD −)

109   Juvenile Courts never give a kid a break.
(− SA, A/ U, D, SD +)

81   Juvenile Courts place kids on probation in order to help them.
(+ SA, A/ U, D, SD −)

COURTS—LEGITIMACY (CR = .91)

106   Juvenile Courts have no right to take kids away from their homes.
(− SA, A, U, D/ SD +)

91   "Who you know" is what counts in the Juvenile Court.
(− SA, A, U, D/ SD +)

64   Juvenile Courts are necessary in our way of life.
(+ SA, A/ U, D, SD −)

82   I would like to be a Juvenile Court judge.
(+ SA, A, U, D/ SD −)

73   Juvenile Courts have too much authority.
(− SA, A/ U, D, SD +)

55   We would be better off if we didn't have any Juvenile Court.
(− SA, A, U/ D, SD +)

99   Juvenile Courts have no right to tell kids what to do.
(− SA, A/ U, D, SD +)

LAWS—RELATIONSHIP WITH KIDS (CR = .93)

92   Laws are harder on kids than on adults.
(− SA, A, U, D/ SD +)

83   Almost everything that is fun for a kid to do is against the law.
(− SA, A, U, D/ SD +)

56   Laws protect the rights of kids.
(+ SA/ A, U, D, SD −)

74   Laws are only made to give kids a hard time.
(− SA, A, U, D/ SD +)

65   The law always works against a kid, never for him.
(− SA, A/ U, D, SD +)

LAWS—LEGITIMACY (CR = .91)

93   Laws should be enforced more strictly.
(+ SA/ A, U, D, SD −)

110   Everyone breaks the law from time to time.
(− SA, A, U, D/ SD +)

100   We would be better off if there were not so many laws.
(− SA, A, U, D/ SD +)

75   Laws are made to be broken.
(− SA, A, U, D/ SD +)

66   It is all right to break the law if you don't get caught.
(− SA, A, U, D/ SD +)

57   There are too many laws.
        (− SA, A/ U, D, SD +)
107   We should obey the law even though
        we criticize it at times.
        (+ SA, A/ U, D, SD −)
84   All laws should be obeyed.
        (+ SA, A/ U, D, SD −)

APPENDIX H

YOUTH DEVELOPMENT PROJECT
INSTRUCTIONS FOR ADMINISTERING INTERVIEW

This schedule is slanted toward the experimental boys. Only two changes, however, are necessary when interviewing the control boys: (1) reword the introductory remarks, which are suggested, so they will be appropriate for the controls, and (2) delete section V from the schedule.

The order of administration will be as follows:

1. Conduct the interview making notes on the schedule.
2. Give the check list to the boy to fill out.
3. While he is doing this, you can fill out the bottom part of this page on the basis of the interview.
4. After the interview, write or record on tape anything you can about the boy that may be useful in writing a report on this follow-up study.

Complete while he is completing the check list

Boy's Name _____ Present School _____

Interviewer's Name _____ Date _____

A. Appearance

    1. Clothing: Neat____ Average____ Disheveled ____

    2. Health: Good ____ Fair ____ Poor ____

3. Personal Cleanliness: Clean _____ Average _____
   Dirty _____

B. Demeanor
   1. Cooperative _____ Average _____ Uncooperative _____
   2. Comfortable _____ Average _____ Uncomfortable _____
   3. Honest _____ Average _____ Dishonest _____
   4. Delinquent _____ Unsure _____ Nondelinquent _____

C. Future Prediction
   1. Finish high school _____ Unsure _____ Dropout _____
   2. Trouble with police _____ Unsure _____ No trouble with police _____
   3. Family adjustment: Good _____ Fair _____ Poor _____

COMMENTS:

YOUTH DEVELOPMENT PROJECT-INTERVIEW SCHEDULE
EXPERIMENTAL BOYS

Suggested introductory remarks:

As part of an assignment at the university, I have decided to talk with all of the boys who were in my seventh-grade class two years ago to find out just how things are going with them in general. You needn't worry about my telling anything you tell me. Whatever we say is just between us.

I. Let's start talking about school. How do you like school? 1 _____ I like it. 2 _____ It's OK. 3 _____ I don't like it.

    a. Why do you (like it, dislike it, or think it's OK)?

    b. Who do you have for English? Is (he-she) (1 _____ easy or 2 _____ hard) to get along with? If *hard*, why?

    c. How about math? Who do you have? Is (he-she) (1 _____ easy or 2 _____ hard) to get along with? If *hard*, why?

    d. How about the rest of your teachers? Are they (1 _____ easy or 2 _____ hard) to get along with? If *hard*, why?

    e. Have you been sent to the office since the beginning of the new semester in February because of being in trouble? 1 _____ Yes 2 _____ No If *yes*, tell me about it. What happened?

    f. Have you cut school since the beginning of the new semester? 1 _____ Yes 2 _____ No If *yes*, how many times? _____ What happened? (Got caught, went to a movie, etc.)

    g. Let's see, you graduate pretty soon. Do you intend to go on to high school?

        1 _____ Yes If *yes*, then what do you think are the chances you will finish? 1 _____ Very good 2 _____ Fair 3 _____ Poor

2 _____ No If *no*, what are you going to do?
4 _____ Get a job 5 _____ Mess around 6 _____
I don't know. 7 _____ Other _____

II. I'm also interested in what you boys do when you're not in school. Let's take after school, for instance. What do you usually do after school? (Lead pupil through sequence of activities.)

   a. Who do you hang around with after school? What do you do?

     Have you gotten in trouble after school since the beginning of the new semester? 1 _____ Yes 2 _____ No If *yes*, tell me about it.

   b. Do you go out after supper? 1 _____ Yes 2 _____ No When you go out, who do you usually hang around with?

     Have you gotten in trouble since the beginning of the new semester when you went out after supper? 1 _____ Yes 2 _____ No If *yes*, tell me about it.

     What time do you usually get home when you've been out after supper? _____

   c. How about during the summer vacation after the seventh grade? Did you have a job or do odd jobs? 1 _____ Yes 2 _____ No If *yes*, what was the job?

     What else did you do that summer? (Probe: who he ran around with, what they did, did he get into trouble?)

How about last summer? After the eighth grade did you have a job or do odd jobs? 1 _____ Yes 2 _____ No If *yes*, what was the job?

What else did you do last summer? (Probe: who he ran around with, what they did, did he get into trouble?)

d. Do you belong to any clubs o r teams or have you received any honors?
1 _____ Yes If *yes*, list below.
2 _____ No If *no*, why?

III. Let's talk about home for a minute. Who lives at home with you?

a. Have you lived with (this-these) (person-persons) all the time since the seventh-grade?
1 _____ Yes 2 _____ No Who else? _____

For *b* through *e* write the name and relationship of each person or group of persons (for example mother, stepfather, grandmother, aunt, cousins, brothers and sisters) in the space provided and get their responses. In general, get the parents or dominant adults' response first, then other persons living with him.

b. Are you getting along better or worse with your _____ (relationship) than when you were in the seventh grade?
1 _____ Better
2 _____ About the same } because
3 _____ Worse

c. How about your _____ (relationship)?
Are you getting along better or worse with
(him-her) than when you were in the seventh
grade?
1 ____ Better ⎫
2 ____ About the same ⎬ because
3 ____ Worse ⎭

d. How about your _____ (relationship)?
Are you getting along better or worse with
them than when you were in the seventh
grade?
1 ____ Better ⎫
2 ____ About the same ⎬ because
3 ____ Worse ⎭

e. How about your _____ (relationship)?
Are you getting along better or worse with
them than when you were in the seventh
grade?
1 ____ Better ⎫
2 ____ About the same ⎬ because
3 ____ Worse ⎭

IV. Is there anything else I should know about you to
help me know how things are going for you?

V. Now let's talk about the seventh-grade class I
taught. Tell me honestly what you thought about
it. Level with me.
a. Are you glad you had this different kind of
seventh-grade class?
1 ____ Yes ⎫ why?
2 ____ No ⎭

b. Think about the fellows you hang around with. Do you feel that any of these fellows could have benefited from this kind of class?

1 ____ Yes

2 ____ No } Why?

c. Do you feel this kind of class would be good for all seventh-grade boys?

1 ____ Yes

2 ____ No } Why?

d. Would you recommend it for seventh-grade boys and girls together?

1 ____ Yes

2 ____ No } Why?

VI. Have you done anything since September that the police could have picked you up for?

APPENDIX I

In attempting to determine the representativeness of the followed-up and non-followed-up groups of experimental and control subjects, data were obtained on the following 13 variables: sixth-grade average, eighth-grade average, sixth-grade reading achievement and arithmetic achievement scores, sixth-grade attendance ratio, eighth-grade attendance ratio, sixth-grade police contacts (serious and moderate), sixth-grade police contacts (slight), age, IQ, delinquency nomination, race, and family status. Variables designated sixth grade were the most recent measures *prior* to the time (seventh grade) when the special classes were held. Variables designated eighth grade were the most recent measures *prior* to the time (ninth grade) when the follow-up interviews were made.

Of the 13 variables examined in which mean scores could be computed, the experimentals interviewed differed significantly from those not interviewed on all but 3. The latter 3 pertained to pre-program variables (sixth-grade reading, arithmetic achievement scores, and age). On each of the 10 statistically significant measures, the direction of the difference favored the interviewees. Thus, they had higher sixth- and eighth-grade school averages, better attendance records, and fewer police contacts, both serious and moderate, and slight (see table I1).

Perhaps the most striking difference between the two experimental groups—interviewees and noninterviewees—was in their racial composition. Nonwhites constituted 61% of the interviewees, 50% of all experi-

TABLE II

Mean Scores of the Follow-up and Non-follow-up Experimentals from the 1964–65 Cohort

Variable	Experimentals						P*
	Follow-up Group			Non-follow-up Group			
	Number of Cases	Mean	Standard Deviation	Number of Cases	Mean	Standard Deviation	
6th-grade grade average†	119	3.14	.71	98	3.43	.85	<.01
8th-grade grade average	118	3.57	.61	66	3.91	.74	<.01
6th-grade reading achievement	117	5.89	1.38	98	5.74	1.48	>.20
6th-grade arithmetic achievement	118	6.42	1.24	99	6.18	1.44	>.20
6th-grade attendance ratio‡	118	.95	.05	99	.92	.07	<.01
8th-grade attendance ratio	118	.94	.06	66	.88	.10	<.001
Delinquency nomination§	120	4.21	2.03	99	4.90	2.21	<.02
IQ‖	120	93.53	12.77	97	91.82	12.89	>.20
Age#	120	13.18	.75	99	13.42	.84	<.05
6th-grade police contacts; serious, moderate	120	.14	.47	99	.40	.85	<.01
6th-grade police contacts; slight	120	.02	.20	99	.14	.38	<.01
8th-grade police contacts; serious, moderate	119	.15	.40	83	.52	1.06	<.01
8th-grade police contacts; slight	119	.06	.30	83	.24	.57	<.02

* Based on the critical ratio of the difference between means.

† A = 1.0, B = 2.0, C = 3.0, D = 4.0, and F = 5.0. This average applies to grades in English, mathematics, and industrial arts only.

‡ Computed by dividing the number of days present by the total number of days for that school year.

§ Nominations range from 0 through 8. The higher a boy's score, the more likely he will become delinquent, according to predictions made by his sixth-grade teacher and principal.

‖ Most recent score prior to beginning the seventh grade.

At the beginning of the seventh grade.

mentals at intake, and only 37% of the noninterviewees. In other words, they were significantly over-
represented, whereas the whites were significantly
underrepresented among the interviewees. Both whites
and blacks in the respondent group had fewer police
contacts (both serious and moderate, and slight), better school records on all measures, and better family
backgrounds in contrast to the nonrespondents in the
experimental group.

On the other hand the experimental interviewees
were similar to the nonrespondents in terms of familial
characteristics. About half in each group came from
broken homes.

THE CONTROLS

The control respondents, although constituting only
34% of all the controls in the 1964–65 cohort, were
more similar to the control nonrespondents than were
the interviewed and noninterviewed experimentals. Of
the 13 variables on which mean scores could be computed only 1, namely, sixth-grade arithmetic achievement, differentiated the control respondents significantly from the control nonrespondents. Both control
groups were similar in age, IQ, sixth-grade reading
achievement scores, sixth- and eighth-grade point-hour
ratios, attendance ratios, and police contacts (serious
and moderate, and slight). These data are presented
in table I2.

Again, the most interesting aspect of this comparison of interviewees and noninterviewees concerned
the racial composition of the two groups. As in the instance of the experimentals, the control interviewees
were predominately nonwhite and the noninterviewees,
white. In numerical terms, 57% of the control inter-

TABLE 12

MEAN SCORES OF THE FOLLOW-UP AND NON-FOLLOW-UP BAD-BOY CONTROLS FROM THE 1964–65 COHORT

VARIABLE	BAD-BOY CONTROLS						P*
	Follow-up Group			Non-follow-up Group			
	Number of Cases	Mean	Standard Deviation	Number of Cases	Mean	Standard Deviation	
6th-grade grade average†	42	3.23	.78	79	3.44	.90	<.20
8th-grade grade average	42	3.64	.61	48	3.52	.90	>.20
6th-grade reading achievement	42	6.24	1.51	76	5.85	1.60	<.20
6th-grade arithmetic achievement	42	6.90	1.29	78	6.30	1.32	<.02
6th-grade attendance ratio‡	42	.94	.09	79	.93	.06	>.20
8th-grade attendance ratio	42	.92	.09	48	.91	.08	>.20
Delinquency nomination§	42	4.12	2.14	81	4.72	1.96	<.20
IQ‖	42	92.45	13.52	79	93.44	15.36	>.20
Age#	42	13.27	.83	81	13.24	.79	>.20
6th-grade police contacts; serious, moderate	42	.10	.29	81	.24	.67	<.20
6th-grade police contacts; slight	42	.02	.15	81	.06	.29	>.20
8th-grade police contacts; serious, moderate	42	.10	.29	61	.25	.67	<.20
8th-grade police contacts; slight	42	.10	.37	61	.12	.37	>.20

* Based on the critical ratio of the difference between means.

† A = 1.0, B = 2.0, C = 3.0, D = 4.0, and F = 5.0. This average applies to grades in English, mathematics, and industrial arts only.

‡ Computed by dividing the number of days present by the total number of days for that school year.

§ Nominations range from 0 through 8. The higher a boy's score, the more likely he will become delinquent, according to predictions made by his sixth-grade teacher and principal.

‖ Most recent score prior to beginning the seventh grade.

At the beginning of the seventh grade.

viewees were black compared with only 21% of the control noninterviewees. For the 1964–65 cohort as a whole, it will be recalled, precisely one-third of the subjects were black.

This overrepresentation of blacks among the follow-up respondents, both experimentals and controls, indicates the parallel unrepresentativeness of those interviewed. It also suggests, supported by the direction of the mean scores on the quantitative variables, that the black student interviewees were indeed a more highly selected group than the whites interviewees. This is so because, in general, white students showed to advantage in each of the three groups (experimental, control, and comparison) at intake into the study. Thus, when a higher percentage of black follow-up subjects scored more favorably, it can only mean that the black respondents were far superior to the black student group as a whole.

Finally, and again comparable to the experimentals, family status did not vary significantly by follow-up-respondent status. Approximately 49% of the cooperators and 47% of the noncooperators were from broken families.

The limitations of the analysis should therefore be evident. Consciously, or because of their school status, the teacher-interviewers collected data from the clearly superior experimentals and the less obviously superior controls. Both cooperating groups were racially and otherwise atypical, casting considerable doubt about the representativeness of the interview data.

THE FOLLOW-UP EXPERIMENTALS AND CONTROLS

The same types of hard data—demographic, school, and police contact—were obtained on the follow-up boys as on all the others. These data indicate that although the interviewees in each group, experimental and control, were different from the noninterviewees, they were not different from each other at intake into the study in the seventh grade.

Demographic Variables

The 120 experimental and 42 control respondents were about 13.2 years of age at study intake. Of the experimentals, 39.2% were white; of the controls, 42.9%. Roughly half in each group—50.8% of the experimentals, 52.4% of the controls—came from intact-family settings.

School Variables

The sixth-grade IQ-test scores, reading and arithmetic achievements, grade-point averages, and attendance ratios were very similar for the experimental and control interviewees. The mean IQ scores for the experimental and control respondents were 93.5 and 92.5; the mean reading achievement grade levels, 5.89 and 6.24; the arithmetic grade levels, 6.42 and 6.90; the grade-point averages ($A = 1$ and $F = 5$), 3.14 and 3.23; and the sixth-grade attendance ratios, .947 and .935.

The later school data indicate the same trends in each group. First, the mean grade-point averages dropped slightly with time. Second, the attendance ratios also declined, although the control respondents showed slightly less truancy than the experimental respondents. Third, the dropout rate was somewhat greater for the control than for the experimental interviewees (see table 13).

Police Contacts

The official police records before, during, and after the program on the experimental and control subjects in the follow-up study were very similar. Prior to the seventh grade, 12.5% of the experimental interviewees and 11.9% of the control respondents had police records for various infractions. There were no differences during the year of the experimental project, since 10.8% and 9.5% of the treated and untreated interviewees, respectively, experienced police contact. In the

TABLE I3

SCHOOL PERFORMANCE DATA OF THE EXPERIMENTAL
AND CONTROL INTERVIEWEES

	EXPERIMENTALS			CONTROLS		
	Total	White	Black	Total	White	Black
Mean IQ Score....	93.53	98.83	90.12	92.45	98.78	87.71
Achievement Level						
Reading........	5.89	6.42	5.54	6.24	6.91	5.73
Arithmetic......	6.42	6.97	6.05	6.90	7.37	6.54
Grade-Point Average*						
6th grade.......	3.14	3.04	3.19	3.23	3.31	3.18
7th grade.......	3.21	3.19	3.22	3.54	3.58	3.51
Post program...	3.57	3.53	3.60	3.49	3.66	3.33
Attendance Ratio						
6th grade.......	.947	.944	.949	.935	.947	.926
7th grade.......	.948	.940	.954	.944	.946	.943
8th grade.......	.936	.933	.939	.923	.936	.913
9th grade.......	.927	.907	.939	.907	.885	.929
10th grade......	.885	.891	.880	.906	.908	.905
Final School Clearance						
% in school.....	77.5	74.5	79.5	69.0	77.8	62.5
% dropout......	11.7	12.8	11.0	21.4	11.1	29.2
% moved away..	8.3	10.6	6.8	7.1	5.6	8.3
% in custody....	2.5	2.1	2.7	2.4	5.6	0.0

* A = 1, B = 2, C = 3, D = 4, and F = 5.

postprogram period of three years, 36.7% and 40.5% respectively became known to the police. For all periods, there were police notations on 43.3% of the experimental (treated) follow-up subjects, and 54.7% of the control (untreated) follow-up subjects.

The preceding analyses have shown two things. First, no matter how measured, the interviewees were self-selected and consequently superior to the noninterviewees on most measures. Second, the two groups of interviewees did not differ from each other on the various demographic, school, and police-contact variables either before, during, or after the Youth Development Project year (seventh grade).

APPENDIX J

SELF-REPORT INSTRUMENT*

(N-S)   1. How often have you driven
(B)   a car without a driver's
*   license or permit? Do
           not include driver training
           courses.)
           3 = very often
           2 = several times
           1 = once or twice
           0 = never

(G)   2. How often have you tried
           to stop a fight?
           0 = very often
           1 = several times
           2 = once or twice
           3 = never

(N-S)   3. How often have you skipped
(B)   school without a legitimate
*   excuse?
           0 = never
           1 = once or twice
           2 = several times
           3 = very often

(B)   4. How often have you dis-
           obeyed your parents?

NOTE: Directionality—low score favorable, high score unfavorable. (N-S) = Nye-Short Items. (G) = "Good" items. (B) = "Bad" items (all "B" items except nos. 4 and 7 are contained in the Nye-Short self-report instrument). (*) = Significant items.

SELF-REPORT INSTRUMENT—(*continued*)

3 = very often
2 = several times
1 = once or twice
0 = never

(G)   5. How often have your refused
*   to smoke?

3 = never
2 = once or twice
1 = several times
0 = very often

(B)   6. How often have you had
     a fist fight with another
     person?

0 = never
1 = once or twice
2 = several times
3 = very often

(B)   7. How often have you told
     a lie?

3 = very often
2 = several times
1 = once or twice
0 = never

(G)   8. How often have you gone
     out of your way to help
     someone?

0 = very often
1 = several times
2 = once or twice
3 = never

(B)   9. How often have you "run
     away" from home?

SELF-REPORT INSTRUMENT—*(continued)*

0 = never
1 = once or twice
2 = three or four times
3 = five or more times

(B)   10. How often have you been placed on school probation or suspended from school?

0 = never
1 = once or twice
2 = three or four times
3 = five or more times

(G)   11. How often have you refused to join the boys in destroying or damaging property?

3 = never
2 = once or twice
1 = several times
0 = very often

(N-S)   12. How often have you defied
(B)   your parents' authority
*   (to their face)?

0 = never
1 = once or twice
2 = several times
3 = very often

(B)   13. How often have you driven
*   too fast or recklessly in an automobile?

3 = very often
2 = several times

SELF-REPORT INSTRUMENT—(*continued*)

          1 = once or twice
          0 = never

(G) 14. How often have you attempted to dress well?
          0 = very often
          1 = several times
           2 once or twice
          3 = never

(N-S) 15. How often have you taken
(B)   little things (worth less
*   than $2) that did not belong to you?
          0 = never
          1 = once or twice
          2 = several times
          3 = very often

(B) 16. How often have you taken
*   things of medium value (between $2 and $50)?
          3 = very often
          2 = several times
          1 = once or twice
          0 = never

(B) 17. How often have you taken
*   things of large value (over $50)?
          0 = never
          1 = once or twice
          2 = several times
          3 = very often

(G) 18. How often have you convinced someone to return stolen property?

3 = never
2 = once or twice
1 = several times
0 = very often

(B) 19. How often have you taken things that you really didn't want that did not belong to you?

0 = never
1 = once or twice
2 = several times
3 = very often

(B) 20. How often have you taken
* part in "gang fights"?

0 = never
1 = once or twice
2 = three or four times
3 = five or more times

(G) 21. How often have you had a date?

0 = very often
1 = several times
2 = once or twice
3 = never

(B) 22. How often have you taken a car for a ride without the owner's knowledge?

0 = never
1 = once or twice

2 = three or four times

3 = five or more times

(B) 23. How often have you "beat up"
* on kids who hadn't done anything to you?

3 = very often

2 = several times

1 = once or twice

0 = never

(G) 24. How often have you offered to
help at home or do something
to help your family?

3 = never

2 = once or twice

1 = several times

0 = very often

(N-S) 25. How often have you bought or
(B) drunk beer, wine, or liquor
* (include drinking at home)?

0 = never

1 = once or twice

2 = several times

3 = very often

(B) 26. How often have you hurt
* or inflicted pain on
someone else just to see
him squirm?

0 = never

1 = once or twice

2 = several times

3 = very often

SELF-REPORT INSTRUMENT—*(continued)*

(G)   27. How often have you
*   studied really hard for
           school work?

    0 = very often
    1 = several times
    2 = once or twice
    3 = never

(N-S) 28. How often have you pur-
(B)   posely damaged or de-
*   stroyed public or private
           property that did not
           belong to you?

    3 = very often
    2 = several times
    1 = once or twice
    0 = never

(B)   29. How often have you used
           or sold narcotic drugs?

    0 = never
    1 = once or twice
    2 = three or more times
    3 = five or more times

(G)   30. How often have you been
*   really nice to one of
           your teachers?

    3 = never
    2 = once or twice
    1 = several times
    0 = very often

(G)   31. How often have you convinced
           someone not to cheat?

SELF-REPORT INSTRUMENT—(*continued*)

0 = very often
1 = several times
2 = once or twice
3 = never

(B)   32. How often have you gone
hunting or fishing without
a license (or violated other
game laws)?

0 = never
1 = once or twice
2 = several times
3 = very often

(G)   33. How often have you read a book
other than one for school?

0 = very often
1 = several times
2 = once or twice
3 = never

Index

INDEX